YORKSHIRE MOORS AND DALES

Text by
MARIAN SUGDEN

Photographs by
ERNEST FRANKL

DILLONS
THE BOOKSTORE

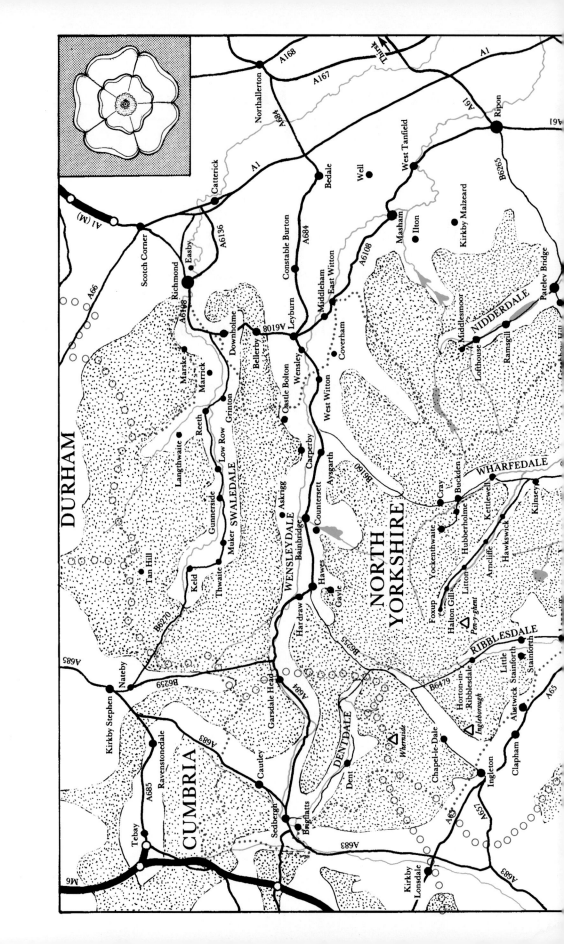

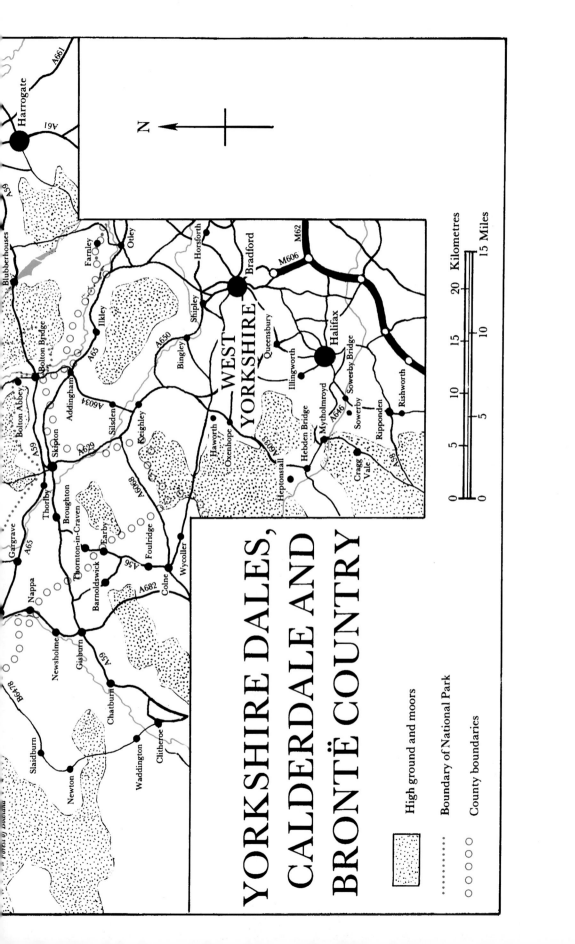

YORKSHIRE DALES, CALDERDALE AND BRONTË COUNTRY

High ground and moors

Boundary of National Park

County boundaries

This edition was produced for Dillons Bookstores by The Pevensey Press

Copyright © 1993 Ernest Frankl, The Pevensey Press

Photographs: Ernest Frankl, except 7: Fitzwilliam Museum, Cambridge

Maps by Carmen Frankl

Quotations: p.28: *The Countryside Companion* (p.192, Wynford Vaughn Thomas, Century Hutchinson, 1979; p.29: *The Best Poems of 1943*, Thomas Moult (ed.), Jonathan Cape, 1944; pp.59 and 62: title and first line of 'Where Millstone Grit and Sky', and lines from 'Wild Rock', *Remains of Elmet*, Ted Hughes and Fay Godwin, Faber and Faber, 1979

The assistance of Alexander Goehr, Robert Muir Wood, Sandra Raban, Dorothy Thompson and Tom Winnifrith is gratefully acknowledged

A catalogue record for this book is available from the British Library.

ISBN 0 907115 75 6

Design by Book Production Consultants, Cambridge
Printed in Hong Kong by Wing King Tong Co. Ltd
for David & Charles plc
Brunel House Newton Abbot Devon

The Pevensey Press is an imprint of David & Charles plc

Front cover
North of Stainforth, Ribblesdale

Back cover
Sheep on Downholme Moor, Swaledale; the stepped roof line of Frenchgate, Richmond; the Strid; the bridge at Arncliffe in Littondale

Title page inset
Hardraw Force, a spectacular waterfall two miles north of Hawes in Wensleydale. The ravine leading to the fall was a favourite place for brass-band contests in the later 19th century – undoubtedly an unforgettable experience in such a setting.

Contents

The Yorkshire Dales: an introduction

The five principal rivers of the Yorkshire Dales – the Aire, Ribble, Swale, Ure and Wharfe – rise in the high Pennines, the backbone of England, in some of the most remote and most dramatic scenery in England. Of these, the Ribble is the only one running to a western outlet. Its broad valley is dominated by three great isolated peaks, Whernside, Ingleborough and Pen-y-ghent, each standing well over 2000 feet above sea-level, a challenge to intrepid fell walkers who race to cover all three within one day. Here also is the potholers' paradise, a vast underground cavernous world of considerable danger and rewarding beauty, much of it as yet unexplored. (See map on front endpapers.)

To the other side of the Pennine watershed the rivers flow generally south-eastward, eventually to converge in the Vale of York and the Humber estuary. The Ure, sometimes spelt Yore, forms the valley of Wensleydale, a name which has obtained for many centuries; the village of Wensley was once an important market town.

Many tributary rivers have carved out smaller dales, each with its own special private character and charm. Two of these are included here: Nidderdale, between the Ure and the Wharfe, and in the far north-west Dentdale, whose river Dee has its source close to that of the Ribble.

The Dales were sculpted by glaciers in geologically recent times. The slow, remorseless ebb and flow of the Ice Age (which came to an end about 10,000 years ago) deposited debris of rock and clay in moraines, banks and barriers, producing the lumpy outlines of valley bottoms and the narrow outlets of branch dales. Valley floors which are flat (e.g. at Kilnsey in Wharfedale) are evidence of post-Ice-Age lakes, and are especially fertile.

The region is of a geological complexity which can only be touched upon here, although the geology accounts for everything that we see. The most palpable contrast is between the sternness of black millstone grit and the brightness of the high limestone – the change from the one to the other strikes clearly and suddenly as we progress up a dale. Perfect limestone country, all blue, green and white in fine weather, has a joyfulness about it unmatched anywhere. In describing his quest in Wharfedale for the rare bird's eye primrose (*In a Green Shade*, 1983), Richard Mabey remarks on the astonishing quickening that limestone brings to a landscape, with sharper colours, more exhilarating air, and even the birds more hectic than elsewhere. In addition, the multi-decker sandwiches of limestone, sandstone and shale known as the Yoredale Series account for much of the terraced appearance of hillsides (**8**). A narrow belt of younger magnesian limestone running north–south at the eastern edge of our area provides a particularly good building material (e.g. at Richmond), as does millstone grit.

1 *The 24-arched Ribblehead Viaduct carries the Settle–Carlisle line, the finest scenic railway in England. The stations which served the villages along the line are now closed, except for special trains, and the viaduct has been threatened with demolition. The church in the tiny hamlet of Chapel-le-Dale has a memorial to the men who died during the building of the viaduct and Blea Moor Tunnel (1869–76).*

1

Ancient upheavals produced geological faults which have created some of the most spectacular of Dales scenery. The Craven Fault, with its cliffs and rugged rocky scars, extends from west of Settle as far as Pateley Bridge in Nidderdale. The cynosure of this system is the sheer cliff of Malham Cove (**3**), whose height of nearly 300 feet surpasses that of Niagara Falls, a mere 167 feet. But the water has gone underground, as is often the way in limestone country, and we are left to imagine the thunderous falls which produced such a precipice.

Our survey of the Dales country covers the area bounded by the borders of Cumbria and Lancashire to the west, and to the east a line from Richmond in the north, through Ripon and Knaresborough, to Ilkley in the south. The line is not entirely notional, for much of it follows the Great North Road (A1), originally a Roman road from London to Scotland. Anyone turning west into Wharfedale or Wensleydale, for example, soon becomes aware of different and delectable country, green and prosperous in its lower reaches – truly a land of milk and honey, each dale distinct and set apart by confining hills, its river winding through long-cherished park- and farmlands. These give way, in some dales quite suddenly, to the open rocky hillsides and small settlements of the narrow upper valleys, a ubiquitous network of dry-stone walls (**2**), and then the ever-changing skyline of high fells and moorland.

In these remote upland fastnesses were the first human settlements of the post-glacial period. Indeed, the hills of western Yorkshire testify to occupation throughout prehistoric times. In the earlier part of the Bronze Age, around 1500 BC, trade in metals and jet was carried on between Ireland and northern Europe, crossing the Pennines via the Aire and Stainmore Gaps. The Brigantes, a tribe of the ancient British, constructed their great Iron-Age hill forts during the 1st

2 *Dry-stone wall repaired with wire to deter athletic sheep and visitors. This network of walls across the hillside, characteristic of the Dales, was photographed just below Middlesmoor, in upper Nidderdale.*

3 *Malham Cove is the most dramatic point in the Craven Fault, the line of craggy cliffs and scars which crosses the Dales from Settle in Ribblesdale to Pateley Bridge in Nidderdale. Waters which once cascaded stupendously over this sheer cliff of nearly 300 feet have disappeared underground. The Aire rises near Malham Tarn, above the Cove.*

century AD, and many traces of them can still be seen (e.g. Lea Green, near Grassington). Their territory stretched right across the north of England, and their opposition to the Roman invaders was long and vigorous.

The Romans built a main road between their fortresses at Aldborough (*Isurium Brigantum*) and Ilkley (*Olicana*); it connected with Manchester by a formidable route over Blackstone Edge (see Calderdale). Another east–west route passed through Wensleydale, where the main fort was at Bainbridge (*Virosidum*), held by the Romans until the end of their rule in the 5th century AD. A long series of invasions and settlements followed, first by the Anglo-Saxons, who were well established over a great part of western Yorkshire by the end of the 6th century, and later by the Danes, who took control of the whole of Eastern England and captured York in 867. Many place-names indicate their gradual and frequently bloody incursions into the Dales, as they cleared woodland and set up their villages along the valleys: *wike* or *wick* is Anglo-Saxon for dwelling place or dairy farm, and Danish (or Norse) names and suffixes such as *-thwaite* (a clearing or meadow) and *-by* (a farm or village) are widespread.

Like the Romans almost a millennium before them, the Normans left little mark on the Dales. But the great monastic foundations which followed the Norman hegemony were to be of lasting significance to Yorkshire and to the Dales, for the

Cistercians were the first to recognise and exploit the natural resources of virgin grassland and water for the production of wool, a prime industry almost to the present day. Foreign trade during the Middle Ages was first and foremost in wool – 'wool was in those times, in truth, the Bank of England' (John James, *History and Topography of Bradford*, 1841). By the end of the 13th century Fountains Abbey was the largest wool producer in the north, and possessed an estimated one million acres stretching right to the borders of Lancashire. Its wool was considered better than any other, and was a lucrative export to the Flemings and Florentines. The business of wool-growing in the Dales developed as a kind of ranching, with a system of granges or outlying homesteads and hamlets belonging to the abbey and connected by still traceable drove roads. The main work-force consisted of lay brothers, probably numbering 500–600 men semi-committed to the monastic life, who lived out in the granges for most of the year.

The spiritual authority of the abbots was matched by often ruthless commercial acumen, preferring sheep to people. R.A. Donkin (*The Cistercians*) quotes contemporary accounts: 'They raze villages and churches . . . and level everything before the ploughshare, not scrupling to grow crops'; the white monks 'frightened the poor and drove them from their land'. Little wonder that abbots and others in positions of power were cast as villains in the popular Robin Hood balladry of the time. The improbable and entertaining tale in which Robin Hood and his men make a trial of strength with the Curtal Friar (whose 100 dogs have the singular ability to catch flying arrows in their mouths; it is nearly an equal contest and ends merrily) is one such poem, set in Fountains Dale or Skelldale, a branch of Wensleydale. Many indications suggest that the folk hero belongs to Yorkshire rather than to Sherwood and Nottingham, and that he, and perhaps many like him,

4 *Sheep have been of prime importance in Yorkshire ever since the great abbeys of the Middle Ages organised their vast wool-growing industry. The dark-faced Swaledale breed, developed centuries ago from the horned or mountain sheep, is unaffected by rough weather and is therefore ideally suited to the fells.*

5 *Easby Abbey, a mile east of Richmond, is close beside a lovely stretch of the Swale. This Premonstratensian foundation dates from c. 1150, and is well preserved, with the windows of the refectory range remaining to their full height. The -by suffix, meaning farm or village, frequently occurs in place-names and indicates a Danish origin.*

roared with bravado like highwaymen up and down the Great North Road and over into Lancashire from their headquarters in the Barnesdale Forest near Pontefract.

During the 14th century the monasteries' prosperity declined, owing partly to recession and financial mismanagement (the development of a futures market in wool would bring debt in the wake of a bad year) and partly to political upheaval. Even so, their wealth constituted an irresistible temptation for Henry VIII, who dissolved the monasteries (1536–9) and sold their lands to such predatory baronial families of the north as the Scropes, Cliffords and Percys.

The popular rising known as the Pilgrimage of Grace was a protest against this, for the ruthless new enclosures practised by the feudal families made the monks seem beneficent by comparison. Its leader, Robert Aske, of Gilling near Richmond, led the rebels to capture York in October 1536, and moved on to Doncaster with a force of thirty thousand. Believing that a pardon was forthcoming from the King, Aske persuaded them to disperse; he was lured to London, tried for treason and hanged in York in 1537.

The Rising of the North, or Earls' Rising (1569), had no such popular support, but was a conspiracy of northern aristocrats against Elizabeth I and in favour of the Roman Catholic Mary Queen of Scots, at that time a prisoner in Bolton Castle, Wensleydale (see p.40). It was nipped in the bud at a single armed encounter at Barnard Castle (north-west of Richmond), and the earls speedily retreated into Scotland. The Queen declared martial law, exacting terrible retribution in the Dales with her demand for at least 700 executions. The victims of this purge were, as a contemporary account said, 'wholly of the meanest sort of people', so that hardly a village escaped the sight of a public hanging.

5

The 17th century brought change, and proliferation of every kind of religious sect. Since the established Anglican church tended to neglect places like the Dales where there were few rich benefices, the ground was fertile for the new forces of Puritanism to take root. Compelling preachers like George Fox (1624–91), who founded the Quakers, met with an enthusiastic response (see Dentdale). A century later, in 1767, John Wesley was to write in a letter to his brother Charles, 'the North of England suits me best, where so many are groaning after full redemption'. Nowhere were his many tireless missionary journeys more successful than in the Dales.

Wesley was appreciative of the Dales country, but found the mountains 'horrid' – a reaction he shared with earlier travellers through the north such as Celia Fiennes, who recorded her journeys in 1697–8, and Daniel Defoe (see p.59). The mid-18th century brought visitors educated by the Grand Tour, seeking the Italianate Picturesque in precipice, gnarled tree and craggy ruin. They were not disappointed. In 1799 William Wordsworth walked through Wensleydale with his sister Dorothy, and in a letter to Coleridge gave a beautiful account of the detour they made to Hardraw Force; his long poems 'The Force of Prayer' (the story of the founding of Bolton Abbey) and 'The White Doe of Rylstone' were written after a visit to Wharfedale a few years later.

J.M.W. Turner (1775–1851), greatest of all English painters, made many visits to Farnley Hall (see p.58) between 1797 and 1818, when he was at the height of his powers. A storm seen from Farnley was a study for his famous painting of Hannibal crossing the Alps, and his painting of Bolton Abbey (now in the Lady Lever Gallery, Merseyside) became famous through being owned by Ruskin, who in *Modern Painters* wrote about the Wharfedale scene with as much felicity as

6 *Swiftly moving clouds create a striking pattern of light and shade over the hills between Hawes in Wensleydale and Kettlewell in Wharfedale.*

Wordsworth about Hardraw. Engravings of Turner's pictures were to make the Dales familiar to a wider English public.

Organised tourism had its first modest beginnings in the Victorian age, helped by new turnpike roads, and given an enormous boost with the coming of the railways. Important old Dales industries such as lead-mining and flax-spinning were in decline and soon to disappear for ever; the woollen industry was transformed by mechanisation and the rapid development of the great south Yorkshire cities. No longer could a whole dale be found where men, women and children were occupied in knitting (all the worsted stockings for the British army in the Napoleonic wars came from the Dales), nor homesteads in which weaving provided half the income and farming the other half. The isolation of centuries was breaking down, and the Dales were gradually becoming valued as a place of rest and recreation for Yorkshire city dwellers – easy of access, and requiring no more than a shilling or so for bus or train, and shoes strong enough for walking. For while ample opportunities may be found for fishing, caving, or pony trekking, this is *par excellence* walking country, whether you are inclined to stroll beside a river from village to village, or to take to the hills and high places (which demand stamina and some preparation).

Two long walks pass through the area, both signposted by their distinctive plain brown wooden markers. The Pennine Way, at 250 miles the longest continuous public walk in England, goes through fairly rough country from Edale in Derbyshire to Kirk Yetholm in Scotland. The completion of the English section of the Way in 1965 was celebrated by a meeting of 2000 enthusiasts on Malham Moor. The route goes through the Dales from Gargrave to Tan Hill.

The Coast to Coast Way, from St Bees Head in the west to Robin Hood's Bay in

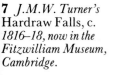

7 *J.M.W. Turner's Hardraw Falls, c. 1816–18, now in the Fitzwilliam Museum, Cambridge.*

the east, is not an official route like the Pennine Way but uses existing rights of way and common land. The splendid Wainwright, whose books are the first requirement in the pocket of every hill walker, reckons that 'for sustained beauty, variety and interest it puts the Pennine Way to shame'. It crosses the Dales through Swaledale.

The 1769 square kilometres (680 square miles) of the Dales National Park, designated in 1954, embraces the upper reaches of all the main rivers with the exception of the Nidd, which lies outside its boundary. The Countryside Commission is responsible for the protection of this area of outstanding natural beauty – maintenance of footpaths, creation of nature reserves and provision of information services. There are six excellent National Park Centres, at Aysgarth Falls, Clapham, Grassington, Hawes, Malham and Sedbergh.

8 *Limestone terracing in Littondale, between Arncliffe and Kilnsey. This recurrent geological feature of the Dales is particularly prominent here.*

The Yorkshire Dales: a gazetteer

Airedale

See map on following page

9 *A solitary barn in Littondale, with evening light catching the typical horizontal lines of long thin stones standing proud, like the 'through' stones of field walls. In some parts of the Dales almost every field has such a barn.*

Upper Airedale, part of the district known as Craven, runs from Skipton, 'gateway to the Dales', to the source of the river beside Malham Tarn, a distance of about 10 miles. The unique landscape of the Malham area (**10**) is deservedly renowned, the more so by contrast with the industrial conurbations of the lower dale (of which more in the second section of this book). It is extremely popular, so every opportunity should be seized for a visit out of season, although it is also a good starting point for excellent hill walks at any time of the year, away from the crowds in a matter of minutes, and offering incomparable views. Some routes follow the old green drove roads (such as Mastiles Lane, which links Malham with Kilnsey in Wharfedale), for this has always been great sheep country, ever since the whole district was divided between the abbeys of Bolton and Fountains.

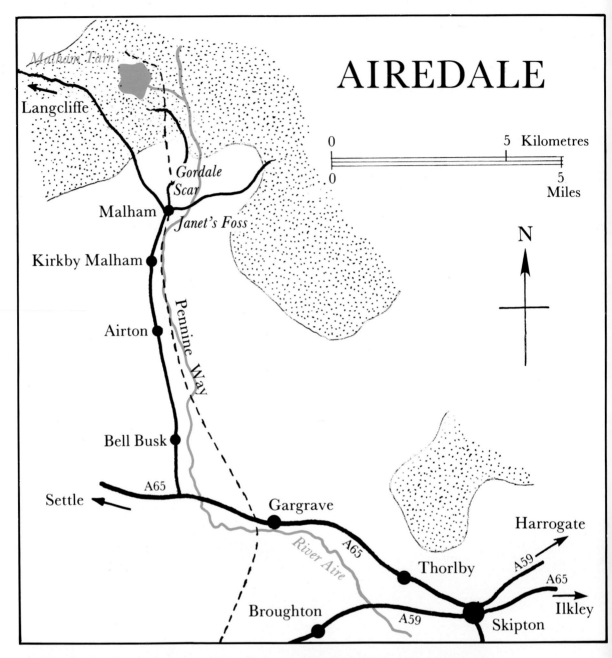

These roads are walled on either side to prevent sheep from straying on to enclosed fields, and everywhere in the parish of Malham the dry-stone walls are its most characteristic feature, evidence of long hard labour which seems to a modern eye well-nigh incredible. Stone-littered hillsides provided material ready to hand, so that wall-building would entail the secondary function of clearing a field; limestone tends to come small and irregular, so that walls here were built thicker than in gritstone areas, and have a haphazard, less finished appearance. A properly made dry-stone wall has big stones top and bottom and at intervals along its height; these so-called throughs serve to strengthen the wall by keeping the smaller stones – fillings – in place. In some areas the throughs project, making a sort of rough pattern, and providing rudimentary steps or a stile. Dry-stone walling is not quite a dying craft; a few professionals exist, and voluntary interest is encouraged.

Nearest the villages the walls mark the modest holdings of old homesteads, and spreading out from these the irregular lines of the 'intakes' show how the farms expanded. A similar pattern is found high on Malham Moor, where the medieval monks had a grange and sheepfolds. The fine, regular walls that swoop up the hillsides are those of 18th-century enclosures. Nowadays it is not uncommon to find walls supplemented by posts and wire, for modern breeds of sheep will jump over almost anything when left to their own devices.

In the present century the Moor has seen some great gatherings. A correspondent remembers hundreds of people camping out all night in 1927 in order to have the best view in England of a total eclipse of the sun.

Airton   The Friends' (Quaker) Meeting House (1700) on the village green, with a small graveyard behind, was founded by William and Alice Ellis, whose own home is opposite and bears their intials WAE (1696). He was a linen weaver who went on preaching missions to America.

Gordale Scar   A short walk from Malham village. Thought to have been formed by a series of fallen caverns. Its ominous overhanging crags and torrential waterfalls have ever appalled and fascinated in equal measure, the shock and menace all the greater for being encountered so suddenly as one turns in from the greenest and most peaceful of meadows.

In a letter of 13 October 1769 to Dr Wharton, the poet Thomas Gray wrote that 'From its very base it begins to slope forwards over you in one black and solid mass without any crevice in the surface, and overshadows half the area with its dreadful canopy...' It has proved an unyielding challenge to artists, including

10 *The Aire near Malham.*

Turner and John Piper. Most ambitious of all was James Ward (1769-1819), whose vast painting hangs in the Tate Gallery in London.

Janet's Foss, another beautiful waterfall close by, is less interrupted than that of the Scar, and has a kindlier setting.

Kirkby Malham   Centre of the upper dale, this village formerly had a busy corn mill and a small cotton-spinning industry. There was a church here in Danish times; the present building is 14th century, considerably restored in the 1870s. Inside are an 11th- or 12th-century circular font, 17th-century family pews, Georgian box pews, and niches whose statues have been destroyed, possibly in Cromwellian days. Stocks near the lychgate.

Malham   has a wide main street and a few attractive houses of historical interest: Priors Hall farmhouse is on the site of a Bolton Abbey grange; the reading room and Beck Hall are on former Fountains Abbey property. The Malhamdale Show takes place here every August.

The road forks in the middle the village, left for the spectacular Cove (**3**), and right for Gordale Scar. Above and beyond these stretches Malham Moor, the lovely tarn, and the mysterious source of the Aire, which disappears into the ground, such is the solubility of limestone. Yet there are records of waterfalls over the Cove in the 19th century, and of their being frozen some time in the 18th. A place of particular geological and botanical interest where the limestone pavements, large weather-beaten flat-topped rocks (clints) riven with deep narrow chasms (grikes), harbour rare flora, even some which may be pre-Ice Age. Charles Kingsley's novel *The Water Babies* was inspired by the country around the Cove and contains beautifully exact descriptions of it.

Skipton   Historically of strategic importance, commanding E–W routes through the Pennines via the Aire Gap. The Honour of Skipton is frequently referred to in the medieval period, 'Honour' being the legal description of a lordship of two or more manors under the control of one baron, or subject to a single jurisdiction; Middleham and Richmond are others. Skipton has always been a site of

11 *The formidable gatehouse of Skipton Castle is early 14th century, but its upper part with balustrade and motto was added by the Lady Anne Clifford, mid-17th century. Desormais was the motto of the Clifford family, and means 'henceforth'. Here it faces both ways, a warning to those without and an inspiration to those within. The castle is open to the public.*

12 *Picturesque Conduit Court, Skipton castle, darkened by a great ancient yew tree, has a finely carved coat of arms of the Clifford family above the doorway. Part of it is Tudor, part was built by Lady Anne Clifford. The lead spoutings bear her initials, A.P. (Anne Pembroke), and the date 1659. A steep exterior stair leads to the great hall.*

fortification; it was given to the Romilly family (see p.51) at the Norman conquest, and later came to the powerful northern family of the Cliffords, who made the castle their principal seat among the 5 they possessed.

The most remarkable of the Cliffords was the Lady Anne (1590–1676), famous for the passionate tenacity with which she pursued her right to a vast inheritance. She rebuilt part of Skipton castle (**12**), founded many charities, and in old age was renowned for the formidable journeys she loved to make, in style and scale comparable to the royal progresses of Elizabeth I. Her descendant Vita Sackville West shared her affection for the north country, and wrote in her edition of Lady Anne's diary: 'I love the hills and wild roads that my old sport Lady Anne used to bump over'.

The castle, in excellent repair, has only one Norman tower. Its stupendous round-towered gatehouse (**11**) is 14th century, as is the great wall on the N side, moated by the Eller Beck, a tributary of the Aire. The more domesticated Tudor wing to the right of the gatehouse has typical mullioned windows. Lady Anne was responsible for the balustrade and motto over the entrance. 18th-century room lined with shells in one of the gate towers.

Holy Trinity church is 14th-century Perpendicular, generously proportioned and not over-restored. Grammar school founded in the 15th century. Good local museum and an important collection of books of antiquarian interest, the Petyt Library (1497–1716), housed in the public library. In the High Street, the best pie shops in England.

Dentdale

Wensleydale and Ribblesdale are linked by 14 miles of high road running through empty moorland, and at Newby Head a side road points westwards to Dent, passing under the Dent Head viaduct, where the railway emerges from Blea Moor tunnel en route to Dent station 2 miles further on, the highest station in England, fortified against the winter snows by walls of upended sleepers. After the viaduct the sudden change of scene and scale is greater than at many a boundary between nations: the road, close beside the delightful infant river Dee (**14**), turns north for a mile or so, and then west into the dale, and we are in another country, unfrequented and warm, sheltered by great hills on all sides, dotted with whitewashed farmhouses, softened by hedgerows and ferns, sweet with wild roses and hayfields.

Dent Town, as it used to be known, was the centre of an extensive parish which thrived on dairy farming, corn, spinning and, until the 1920s, the quarrying and finishing of marble. It was notorious, too, before the advent of the knitting machine, for its 'terrible knitters' (as other dalespeople referred to them) – men, women and children who would knit up to 12 woollen caps a day.

Dent sits compact on its low hillside. The main street is entirely and ruggedly cobbled. Strong, square-towered church conceals well-kept woodwork, Jacobean box pews, and a balustraded chancel with floor of local marble. A huge stone erected beside the church gate (**13**) commemorates Dent's most illustrious son, Adam Sedgwick (1785–1873), who became the first Professor of Geology at Cambridge. A memorial within the church tells of his abiding love for his native place – always the first accolade for a Yorkshireman from his compatriots.

Two side valleys should be walked for the experience in microcosm of the variety of Dales scenery, from shaggy woods and singing waters to heights of wild grandeur. Deepdale runs southwards from Dent, by Whernside. The steep, gated road winds its way over into Kingsdale and down into Ingleton. Barbondale lies W of Deepdale and roughly parallel to it.

13 *This drinking fountain, made from a huge block of rough-hewn Shap granite, is a memorial to Adam Sedgwick, first Professor of Geology at Cambridge. It stands near the southern entrance to the churchyard in Dent, where his father was vicar.*

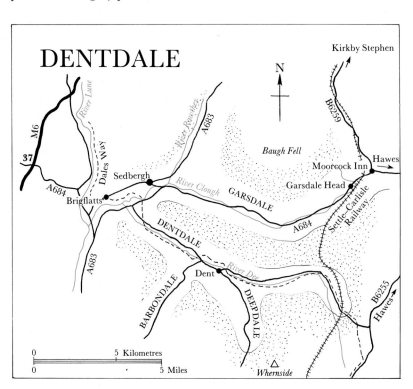

14

Sedbergh, a little town 5 miles NW of Dent, is on the old turnpike road from Lancaster to Newcastle, and at the confluence of three rivers, the Dee, the Clough (which runs through Garsdale) and the Rawthey, whose valley runs NE alongside the high rounded Howgill Fells, the last barrier between Yorkshire and the Lake District. Sedbergh School, founded 1525, is now one of the premier schools of England.

George Fox, founder of the Society of Friends, or Quakers, was well received in these parts when he journeyed north in 1652, preaching to crowds of 1000 or more near Dent and Sedbergh, as well as in the Dales and Craven. On Firbank Fell, W of Sedbergh, an inscription marks a rock where he spoke for three hours to a vast congregation; Brigflatts, SW of Sedbergh, has the first Quaker meeting house in the north of England (1675), and remains a place of pilgrimage for Quakers from all over the world.

14 *A sylvan scene in Dentdale, near Dent Youth Hostel.*

Nidderdale

The green woodlands and dark rocks of Nidderdale encompass many contrasts and curiosities, from eccentric Knaresborough to distant, secret Middlesmoor in the arms of the Whernsides – hills rising to over 2000 feet, bleak and forbidding after the lush pastoral scenes below (not to be confused with the Whernside by Dentdale). The river Nidd passes through a series of reservoirs constructed early this century to serve Bradford: Angram and Scar House, high in the valley, and lower down Gouthwaite, appearing like a mature, natural lake, a rare sight in the Dales.

It is potholing country where the land changes from gritstone to limestone, above Middlesmoor, and there are spectacular caverns open to the public at Stump Cross, by Greenhow, whose hills are strewn with remains of old lead workings. Mining began here in Roman times (the Roman road from Ilkley to Aldborough came right across Nidderdale); the industry reached its peak in the early 19th century, declining rapidly thereafter, and was defunct by 1900 (see Swaledale). Besides quarrying and farming – there was an important export of bacon and butter to London – a busy hemp- and flax-spinning industry flourished in the 18th century, and the remains of the mills and their waterwheels (**18**) punctuate the side valleys.

The Nidderdale Way, signposted for walkers, is a circular route from Hampsthwaite to Scar House reservoir.

Brimham Rocks (National Trust; **16**), easily reached between Pateley Bridge and Ripon, lie in 50 acres of high, heathery moorland commanding grand views of

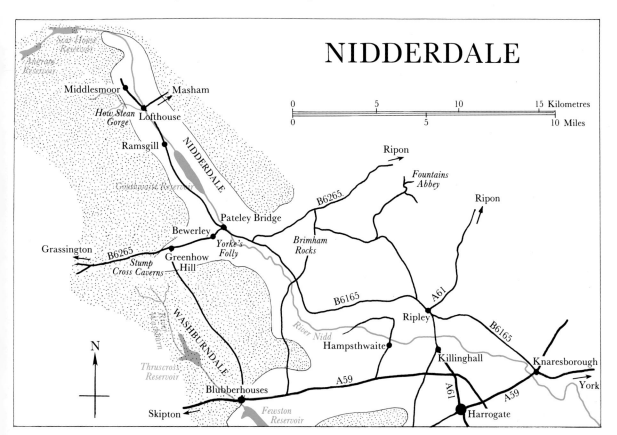

Nidderdale and the Vale of York. The gritstone cap of the hill, sandwiched with more friable stone, was carved by wind and weather during the Permian period (250 million years ago, in a subtropical climate, when most of this land was covered by sea) into the most fantastical pinnacles, stacks and arches. 'There it stands, colossal, half-frowning, half statue, half rock… its colouring is of mellow grey, and moorland moss clothes it, and heath, with its blooming bells and balmy fragrance, grows faithfully close to the giant's foot.' Charlotte Brontë's words (describing literary creation) may give an insight to the work of Yorkshire-born sculptor Henry Moore (1898-1986) perhaps the most internationally acclaimed British artist of this century, who traced his earliest inspiration to rocky outcrops like these, and who described sculpture as a mixture of the human figure and landscape.

It is an awesome place, requiring time, solitude and silence for contemplation.

Greenhow   Reached by a brake-testing lane off the road between Pateley Bridge and Grassington (Wharfedale), this hill village has the second highest parish church in the country. Centre of the old lead-mining area – 'pigs' (oblong blocks) of Greenhow lead have been discovered bearing Roman inscriptions of the 1st century AD. The impressive Stump Cross Caverns, named after the remains of a cross which marked the bounds of the forest of Knaresborough, are well worth a visit. Open daily from Easter to October, they offer the 'thrill and challenge of going underground in comfort and safety, with modern lighting and footpaths'.

Harrogate   'Britain's Floral Town' grew rapidly as a favoured watering place during the 19th century and retains its Victorian essence, graced by elegant shops and wide, tree-lined streets.

The first medicinal spring, discovered long before (1571), is known as Tewit Well, on the Stray (one of the town's many green spaces); a dome and Tuscan columns were added in 1842. Soon after its discovery Harrogate was christened the

15 Harrogate is unusually rich in parks and gardens – this formal display was photographed in Montpelier Gardens.

16 *Brimham Rocks, on a 50-acre National Trust site between Pateley Bridge and Ripon, are gigantic outcrops of gritstone, weatherbeaten through aeons of time into fantastic shapes – some, like this one, suggest prehistoric monsters; others have been described with names such as Dancing Bear or The Elephant.*

English Spa, thus bringing a Belgian place-name into use as a common noun. Subsequently more than 100 springs were found, and were claimed by contemporary developers to possess particular medicinal qualities. 'Taking the waters' is no longer the popular remedy it used to be, although the curious may, if they are bold enough, taste the strong-smelling sulphurous well water on tap in the octagonal Royal Pump Room (1842). Nearby is the imposing building of the Royal Baths (1897), with Turkish-style interiors.

The town's most distinctive feature and the reason for its justified pride is the large number of beautiful greens and gardens (**15**). The Valley Gardens follow a winding stream, exotically planted, and give pleasure at every season: here are formal displays, woodland with pine and rhododendron, a sun colonnade, playgrounds, tennis courts, mini-golf, and an unusually pretty Magnesia Well Refreshment Room, laced with wrought-iron work. In another gentle valley on the edge of the town is the splendid Harlow Car Garden (*car* meaning 'pond' or 'bog'), owned by the North of England Horticultural Society; among many other delights it has alpine houses and water gardens, as well as specialist trial grounds for (e.g.) the National Rose Society and the Heather Society. The Harrogate Spring Show, in April, is an essential date in every gardener's calendar.

The Great Yorkshire (agricultural) Show takes place every July on its permanent ground here; there is also the Harrogate International Festival of music and arts in the summer, and an autumn flower show held in September. The conference centre, a startling drum of white concrete and red brick, practical and much in demand, makes an important contribution to the economy of the town and contrasts with the remaining monolithic hotels, redolent with Edwardian luxury.

17 *The churchyard at Middlesmoor, at the head of Nidderdale. This peaceful place, the site of an Anglo-Saxon settlement, gives a magnificent view of the whole upper dale.*

Shopping is of the most superior order, especially for clothes and antiques. One famous place must be singled out, the irresistible Betty's Cafe. Established in 1919, it keeps the decor of the time, live twenties music is played on a white piano and white-aproned waitresses serve a variety of delicious Yorkshire fare – curd tart, fat rascals, teacakes, bilberry pies, hot milk with honey and nutmeg…

Lofthouse Site of a Fountains Abbey grange; the adjacent moorland is still known as Fountains Earth. Monks from Byland (SW of Helmsley) mined ironstone here. Good walks and fine scenery – to How Stean Gorge nearby, where the How Stean Beck plunges between vertical 70-foot cliffs, or up to the reservoirs of Angram and Scar House.

Knaresborough Exceptionally picturesque, as well as rich in curiosities. The Nidd flows through a deep gorge below sheer cliffs of golden sandstone, overlooked by the ruined remains of the once massive royal castle (mainly early 14th century; its demolition was ordered by Cromwell after the battle of Marston Moor, see p.22). Houses have been crammed against its walls and perched precariously on the sides of the ravine, and even carved into the rock. The House in the Rock (1770), off Abbey Street, is sometimes open to visitors; here also is the tiny chapel of Our Lady of the Crag (founded 1409) with the surprising, larger-than-life-size statue of St Robert of Knaresborough, a local hermit, depicted in full armour. The 'Oldest Chymist's Shoppe' in England is in the market place. Fine 18th-century houses and bow-windowed shops in the High Street. St John's church, 12th–15th century, has interesting 17th-century monuments and memorials.

The riverside walk, through the Dropping Well estate, is especially fine (entrance on the Harrogate side of the High Bridge). At the start of the walk one looks up to a crazy skyline of roofs and chimneys, and across the river to black-

and-white checkerboard-patterned houses, whose colours may be echoed in those of the Muscovy ducks on the water. The scene is overshadowed here by the huge viaduct, 'one of the most notable railway crimes in England', Pevsner says, though not all would agree. In any case it is soon forgotten when one reaches the magnificent stretch of river at the rushing weir and the old mill. Through brightly lichened beech woods, carpeted with bluebells in springtime and wonderfully coloured in autumn, the walk carries on to its strange focus, the Dropping Well, a waterfall possessed of petrifying properties and hung about with an assortment of cast-off clothes and toys in various stages of wet, brown stoniness. Then one comes to Mother Shipton's Cave, a small, dark, mercifully dry grotto, with coloured lights and a crumbling representation of this witch or prophetess, born in the cave in the late 15th century, and said to have exhibited supernatural powers. She is supposed to have foretold the invasion and defeat of the Spanish Armanda in 1588; and Samuel Pepys' Diary grimly records that Mother Shipton gave forewarning of the Great Fire of London in 1666. Beside the cave, the famous Petrifying Well – a unique geological phenomenon.

Middlesmoor   Last village in the dale, 1000 feet above sea level, on the site of an Anglo-Saxon settlement. Church with Saxon font and cross head. Magnificent views of the whole of the upper dale from the windswept churchyard (**17**), and a rare atmosphere of total peace.

Pateley Bridge   received its Royal Charter in the 14th century. In the 18th and 19th centuries it was the centre for the mining, quarrying and spinning industries of the dale, served by the single-track Nidd Valley Light Railway (dismantled 1936) running from Harrogate to Lofthouse. The town is full of flowers all through the summer. Nidderdale Show in September.

18 Foster Beck Mill, a short distance updale from Pateley Bridge, is now the Watermill Inn. The great wheel of this former hemp mill has been restored as a memento of a past industrial life.

The surrounding hills contain Bronze-Age remains. Yorke's Folly, a striking sight on the hillside to the S, across the river, consists now of two hugh stone piers which John Yorke of Bewerley caused to be built in order to provide employment (at 4 pence a day) during a period of recession in the 18th century; a third and larger tower collapsed in 1893.

Ramsgill The most picturesque village in the dale, set around a green, lies at the head of the Gouthwaite reservoir, a favourite place for bird-watchers – rarities such as kites and golden eagles have been seen here. A quiet bridle path, part of the Nidderdale Way, on the E side of the lake leads down to leafy, secluded Wath (a Norse name meaning a ford) at its S end. Another delightful walk is along the riverside from Ramsgill to Lofthouse.

Ripley Largely a model village created in 1827 by Sir William Ingilby after the pattern of a French village in Alsace. It has preserved its cobbles, ancient stocks, and a market cross – and a certain charm, although nothing to compare with that of any Dales village which has grown in its own slow way over many centuries.

Ripley has belonged to the Ingilby family uninterruptedly since the 14th century. Their castle was much rebuilt in the 18th century, with an elegant orangery in the gardens. Guided tours of the interior, which contains some good Jacobean rooms. Cromwell is said to have stayed here after his victory in the final, decisive battle of the Civil War at Marston Moor (E of Knaresborough) in 1644. Church (where Cromwell reputedly stabled his horses) rebuilt after a landslide *c.* 1395. Upper parts dated 1567. Several Ingilby monuments, the finest a tomb chest of 1369, with reclining effigies of Sir Thomas Ingilby and his wife, and all their little children in delicate carving round the sides. In the churchyard is a unique Weeping Cross. Only the lower portion remains of the shaft; the base plinth has narrow spaces cut into it where penitents would kneel.

Ribblesdale

Markedly apart from the rest of the Dales, Ribblesdale sweeps down, expansive, wide and open between the majestic hills of Pen-y-ghent (2273 feet; **19**) and Ingleborough (2372 feet). The rock is predominantly limestone, which is particularly subject to erosion by rain; on the hillsides the bands of limestone therefore tend to have vertical faces, and are interspersed with sloping screes of the more impermeable sandstone strata. It is the limestone's solubility which causes drainage to flow underground, creating the endlessly fascinating world of the speleologists, who have plotted the subterranean courses of streams by adding chemical dyes. The water emerges on the surface when it leaves the limestone, often at a great distance from where it first disappeared.

Alum Pot, on the north slope of Ingleborough, is one of the most famous potholes. Gaping Gill, on the opposite side, has the highest known (underground) waterfall in England, a vertical shaft of over 360 feet. Near Ingleton, the White Scar Caves are open throughout the summer season, offering guided tours of a magical cave system which includes one of the biggest cave chambers in the country, 700 feet long, known as the Battlefield.

There is little heavy woodland. Limestone supports ash and thorn, hazel and bird cherry, besides a great variety of flora; sturdier trees such as oak find a foothold in the ancient Silurian rock around Ingleton; and sycamores are frequently planted to shelter isolated farms. The green pastures and vast sheep-runs of the dale, shared in medieval times between the abbeys of Sawley (south of Settle) and Fountains, are seen at their best in the frequently uncertain weather on the west of

OVERLEAF
19 *The unmistakable profile of Pen-y-ghent (2273 feet), watching over Ribblesdale near the village of Horton-in-Ribblesdale. Along with Ingleborough and Whernside it comprises the 'Three Peaks' course, which intrepid fell walkers race to complete within 24 hours.*

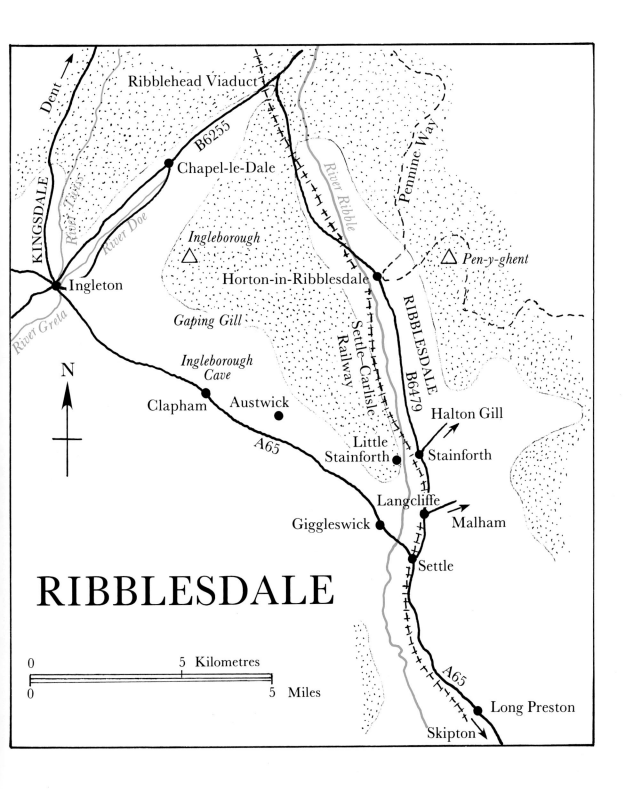

RIBBLESDALE

Ribblehead Viaduct

Dent

KINGSDALE

River Twiss

River Doe

B6255

Chapel-le-Dale

Ingleton

River Greta

River Ribble

Pennine Way

Ingleborough

△

Pen-y-ghent

△

Horton-in-Ribblesdale

Gaping Gill

RIBBLESDALE

B6479

Settle–Carlisle Railway

Ingleborough Cave

N

Clapham

Austwick

A65

Halton Gill

Little Stainforth

Stainforth

Langcliffe

Malham

Giggleswick

Settle

0   5   Kilometres

0   5   Miles

A65

Long Preston

Skipton

the Pennines, when fierce rainclouds racing in from the sea make an ever-changing pattern of dark and light with rainbows across the landscape.

Austwick   Small village of great charm, and a favourite centre for walkers and geologists. On the green, a gastronomically renowned inn, the Gamecock, and a blacksmith's shop. The medieval base of the market cross is a relic of more important times. Outlying terraced fields to the S and W; evidence of Iron-Age settlements in the hills around.

Due N, small, solitary Crummackdale, and above it (SW) Norber Rocks, a remarkable freak of nature – great boulders of ancient Silurian gritstone brought by glacial action and deposited on pedestals of younger limestone.

Chapel-le-Dale   Tiniest of hamlets. The secluded, simple little church has a memorial to the men who died during the construction of the railway (1869-76) which crosses the head of the dale – the Blea Moor Tunnel and the impressive, 24-arched Ribblehead Viaduct (**1**). The stations which served the villages along the line are now closed, except for special trains; however, money has been found to save the viaduct from demolition and efforts to save the route from Settle to Carlisle, the finest scenic railway in England, have proved successful in staving off the initial threat.

Clapham   Attractive village with an unusual abundance of trees. Planting begun

20 *The Shambles, in Settle's market square, is an unusual and striking combination of 17th century (round-headed arches) and late Victorian (houses on the upper gallery).*

in the early 1800s by local landowners, of whom one was the distinguished botanist Reginald Farrer (1880–1920), described as the father of English rock gardening. His garden at Ingleborough Hall was famous in its day. Cherries, limes and hornbeams line the riverside in the middle of the village, and the careful planting continues with new variegated specimens and underplanting of rhododendron. Fine old copper beeches behind the church's medieval tower. A nature trail leads past an artificial lake to Ingleborough Cave, the gorge of Trow Gill, Gaping Gill and eventually to the top of Ingleborough.

Giggleswick   Adjoining Settle, across the Ribble, a distinct and self-contained village with a lovely Perpendicular church dedicated to St Alkelda (a Saxon martyr?). Fine carved pulpit and reading desk (1680). Memorial to Dr George Birkbeck (1776–1841), who was born in Settle and worked to popularise science: he founded the first Mechanics' Institutes, one of which became the London college which bears his name. Giggleswick School founded late 15th century. The A65 from Ingleton to Settle follows the line of the Giggleswick Scar, part of the Craven Fault, a dramatic scene above an unfortunately busy road.

Horton-in-Ribblesdale   Straggling grey village at the foot of Pen-y-ghent. Another much-frequented centre with many good walks, such as the bridle-path (green road) to Upper Wharfedale – the route used by the monks of Jervaulx to their landholdings here – and the Pennine Way. Quarrying all around and down to Helwith Bridge, for slate as well as for limestone. Plain, low-lying Norman church, with Perpendicular tower. Its dedication is to St Oswald, a Northumbrian king who was converted to Christianity in Iona during exile in Scotland, and who died fighting the king of Mercia, AD 642.

Ingleton   Narrow gorges and tumbling waterfalls above the confluence of two rivers, the Twiss (or Dale Beck, coming from Chapel-le-Dale) and the Doe (or Thornton Beck, from Kingsdale), which join to form the Greta, make Ingleton one of the most spectacular and popular beauty spots in all the Dales: the Falls Walk (*c.* 4 miles) starts from near the centre of the village. Church with especially fine Norman font. The advent of the railway in the 1840s, and brief exploitation of coal workings in the early 20th century, have made Ingleton disappointing architecturally, but accommodation is plentiful, with good facilities for camping, fishing, etc. At the top of Ingleborough, *c.* 4 miles NE, remains of Iron-Age hill fort: foundations of huts still visible, and formidable ramparts (partly despoiled in recent times in the construction of a modern cairn).

Langcliffe   N of Settle, a starting point for footpath walks to Malham Tarn, Malham and Arncliffe. The first of these passes Victoria Cave (discovered in 1838, the year after Queen Victoria's accession), which was found to contain prehistoric remains of animals such as woolly rhinoceros and elephant, and artifacts of the Old Stone Age – now housed in the Settle museum.

Settle   Market town and holiday resort, narrow streets rather congested in summer. The Shambles (**20**), facing the market square, is a striking 17th-century building with six round-headed arches and an upper gallery of Victorian houses. A considerable amount of attractive domestic building, doorways with decorated lintels characteristic of this area, and a sizeable house in the High Street, known as the Folly (1679), of such unusual and quirky detail that Pevsner himself is hard put to attempt any classification.

Stainforth   The loveliest stretches of the Ribble are here, including Stainforth Force and Catrigg Force. The steeply hump-backed packhorse bridge on the road to Little Stainforth is a treasure of the National Trust, a fine example of the 17th-century stone-mason's craft. Spectacular drive between Stainforth and Halton Gill (Littondale, see p.57).

Swaledale

This most romantic of dales begins, unlike others, narrow, tortuous and well wooded in its lower reaches. Richmond, capital of the old district (or Honour, see p.12) of Richmondshire, is situated above a deep river gorge, and commands the eastern approach to the dale; it is one of the finest small towns in England.

The valley becomes ever wider as it climbs towards its river source, the watershed of Mallerstang, and Angram Common under Great Shunner Fell (2340 feet), in contrast with the little, secluded valleys of Birk Dale, Whitsun Dale, Stock Dale, and Great and Little Sled Dale. The majesty of upper Swaledale can be best appreciated coming west to east, perhaps approaching through the dramatic Buttertubs Pass from Hawes in Wensleydale (**21**).

'All the fells here are over the 2000-foot level and in autumn the heather dyes them a rich purple. They are rough walking, with patches of sphagnum moss, but the birds are your reward. The curlew calls, the grouse clatter away across the heather. . . The streams tumble down the hillsides in white skeins of waterfalls in the stony clefts or "gills", and the stone walls make subtle patterns against the green lower slopes.' So Wynford Vaughan-Thomas described his first sight of Swaledale in *The Countryside Companion* (1979), and sensed, as he bicycled down, that he 'wasn't simply riding through the splendid scenery but through the very character of the Yorkshire folk – strong and unyielding like their moors above, warm and loyal beneath like their dales'.

It is lonely country, and has suffered steady depopulation over the past two centuries. From 1750 to 1850 the most important industry was lead-mining. Agriculture began to decline in the mid-19th century with the advent of Free Trade and huge imports of Australian wool, and from this time there was considerable emigration, especially to Iowa and Ohio. The railway came to Wensleydale in 1877 but never reached Swaledale, so it largely escaped the first wave of Victorian tourism, and its relative isolation has continued until recent times.

21 *Buttertubs Pass, which links Hawes in Wensleydale to Thwaite in Swaledale, is named after the strangely fluted, 60-foot-deep potholes, close to the roadside. It runs just west of Lovely Seat (2213 feet) and is frequently blocked by snow.*

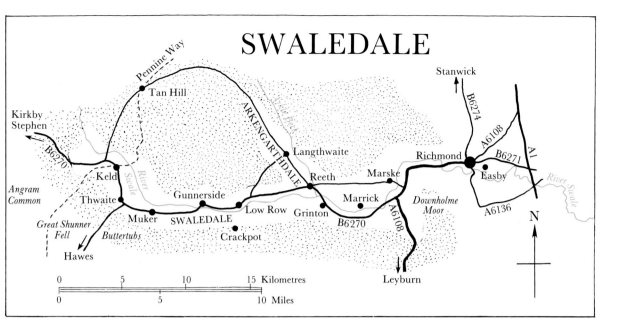

SWALEDALE

Kirkby Stephen · Pennine Way · Tan Hill · Stanwick · Richmond · Langthwaite · Reeth · Marske · Easby · Keld · ARKENGARTHDALE · Gunnerside · Marrick · Angram Common · Thwaite · Low Row · Grinton · Downholme Moor · Muker · SWALEDALE · Crackpot · B6270 · A6108 · A6136 · Great Shunner Fell · Buttertubs · Hawes · Leyburn

0 ... 5 ... 10 ... 15 Kilometres
0 ... 5 ... 10 Miles

N

Arkengarthdale runs NW from Reeth, following the course of the Arkle Beck, through unfenced moorland up to a focal point for drovers coming over from Teesdale and places further N – Tan Hill, at 1700 feet the highest inn in England, where there used to be a great sheep market, and dog racing (and no doubt less innocent entertainments). Beyond the timeless village of Langthwaite are only a few scattered grey hamlets, whose original settlements were Norse (Booze, for example), and all around the exhilaration of pure air and the sound of curlews on the high fells.

> Our maps are music, and they sing the miners'
> Old wrestle with the rocks for yield of lead:
> There's Old Gang, Windegg, Eskeleth, and Crackpot,
> And Racca Vein, forsaken. They are dead.
>
> (Ivor Brown, 'The Moorland Map')

It is difficult now to visualise the dale with its former population of more than 1000. The road from Langthwaite to Low Row passes through the principal lead-mining area, to which hundreds of workers came on foot from their cottages in Swaledale, and from which the lead was carried by packhorse down the dale and eventually south and abroad. The landscape is made desolate by the spreading spoil heaps of the mines, ruined smelting works, and the scars of hushes (where water had been dammed high on a hill, and then released so that its force would scour the soil to reveal a promising mineral vein) – all riches for the industrial archaeologist (**24**).

Easby Best approached by the leisurely mile of riverside walk from Richmond, the way followed by Turner, who was entranced by Swaledale and made some of his loveliest drawings and watercolours here. The abbey (**5**), excellently preserved, and beautifully sited beside the curving river, dates from about 1150; it follows the general plan of Cistercian foundations, but the exigencies of the immediate geography led to intriguing variations (see Pevsner). Most impressive is the refectory range: windows to their full original height, over an undercroft. A plain, round-arched gatehouse lies at some distance from the abbey buildings. Between the two is the church of St Agatha, Early English, with some Perpendicular work (e.g. S porch and S aisle) and some 19th-century restoration; small windows make

OVERLEAF
22 *Sheep on Downholme Moor, south-west of Richmond.*

29

it unusually dark. 13th-century wall paintings (**23**). The Easby Cross was the finest Anglo-Saxon carving in Yorkshire – it is now in the Victoria and Albert Museum in London, but a copy is kept in the church.

Grinton Once the market centre of upper Swaledale. A fair took place every Sunday for all who came from the extensive parish to its only church, a 12th-century foundation with later medieval features, and the curiosity of a 'leper's squint' – a narrow window about 14 inches high, set in an angle of the S wall to provide a view of the altar within, for those who could not be admitted to the church. Until the end of the 16th century the dead were carried here in wicker coffins from the remotest corners of the dale, along a route still known as the Corpse Way.

Gunnerside Norse name meaning pasture land belonging to someone called Gunnar. Big village on a broad hillside cut by Gunnerside Gill, which comes down from Rogan's Seat (2204 feet). Walls in the dale bottom outline irregular ancient enclosures; long straight walls higher up mark common fields divided in the early 19th century. Many small houses in the village belonged to the families who worked the Old Gang and Surrender mines (see p.29).

Keld Norse word for a spring. The last and highest village in the dale, and now one of the smallest. It was a strong Nonconformist centre: the independent chapel, founded at the end of the 18th century, records a congregation of 343 on Christmas Day 1843. The population is now much depleted – a change parallelled in villages all along the dale.

High above a magnificent wooded gorge and skirted by the Pennine Way, Keld provides a starting point for countless explorations, to high fells or to remote side valleys. Many spectacular waterfalls: Kisdon Force, close by; Cartrake Force, less

23 *The 13th-century wall paintings in the chancel of St Agatha's church, in the grounds of Easby Abbey. The upper row depicts the Annunciation to the Shepherds and the Adoration of the Magi; the lower, the Deposition, the Entombment and the Marys at the Sepulchre. The window surrounds have secular scenes such as Harvesting, Pruning and Sowing.*

24 *Upper Swaledale supported a big lead-mining industry, employing hundreds of workers during the 18th and 19th centuries but now completely defunct. Its remains, such as this tunnel entrance near Keld and the lumpy contours of spoil heaps, are still to be seen on the hillsides, and are promising sites for industrial archaeology.*

accessible; Wainwath Falls, beyond Birk Dale, where water was dammed for lead-mining. Surrounding hills bear many traces of lead workings, though none so desolate as those above Low Row. Following the Swale in its upper reaches the road is outstandingly pretty, close to the river chattering along under limestone cliffs.

Marske   Luxuriant parkland with handsome conifers and beeches surrounding a Georgian hall. Stable buildings topped by an unusually high cupola. Church originally Norman, but more interesting for its 17th-century restoration. Fine bridge over the Marske Beck, probably 15th century.

Muker   Attractive close-knit grey village near the river. Mainly 19th-century church, originally a chapel of ease, where services were held for parishioners who could not go all the way to Grinton. The Literary Institute (1868) is a surprising little building with a Dutch gable and a heavy porch, proudly and centrally placed just below the church. A Show and Sports, including a Fell Race, are held here every September. Riverside walks up to Keld and down to Gunnerside.

Reeth   At the centre of the dale, and once a thriving market town. In the heyday of the lead industry the population was three times its present size. Now busy with visitors, and important locally. An agricultural show takes place in August – great flocks of sheep being moved from one pasture to another may hold up traffic as they flow like a river across the wide green. Some good 18th-century houses and inns, plain and unspoilt.

Richmond   One of England's finest towns (**25**), with one of the best of English castles, a splendid sight from the south, across the river: mighty walls above an almost sheer cliff, and an uncompromising keep, dead centre. Founded by a kinsman of William the Conqueror in 1171, as a fortress from which to subdue the

natives, it has played very little part in subsequent political history. Most of the building belongs to the 12th century; the great hall (Scolland's Hall) is probably the oldest in England.

The other significant medieval building is Greyfriars Tower, remains of a 14th–15th-century Franciscan monastery, standing impressively in a bright little park N of the market place, near the Tourist Information Centre.

Richmond's greatest architectural wealth is of the 18th century, in cobbled streets with resonant northern names such as Frenchgate (**26**), Pottergate, Callowgate. The market place is vast and entirely cobbled. Tall obelisk (1771) on the site of the old market cross. Trinity Church is now the museum of the local regiment, the Green Howards. Castle Hill, leading from the market place to the river, brings into view the octagonal Gothick Culloden Tower, built to celebrate the English victory over the Scots in 1746.

Richmond is especially proud of its tiny Theatre Royal (1788), the best preserved and most perfect Georgian theatre in England, restored to its original appearance and use in 1963.

Stanwick   On the edge of the village of Forcett, 9 miles N of Richmond. A series of earthworks constructed to the orders of the heroic British general Venutius against the Roman invaders in the 1st century AD. The banks and ditches were several times extended (AD 50–70) to a final circumference of 6 miles.

Sir Mortimer Wheeler, who excavated a small section of the fortifications in 1951, reached the cut rock base of the earthwork and partially restored some dry walling at a depth of about 30 feet. 'We can almost see the tribesmen toiling vainly at their gate, almost hear the 9th Legion trampling up from its new fortress at York to one of its rare victories.' The site (in the care of the Department of the Environment) is now thickly wooded and utterly peaceful in the midst of cornfields, in sharp contrast to the vivid imaginings of the experienced archaeologist.

25 *Richmond is beautifully and strategically sited above the Swale. It grew up around the castle (founded 1171), whose fine foursquare keep dominates the skyline.*

26 *Frenchgate, Richmond, illustrates the range of architectural pleasure to be found in the town – old stone pavements, cobbled roads, stepped roof lines and calm 18th-century propriety.*

34

Wensleydale

'Yorkshire being the biggest is therefore the best county in England' – words quoted from Thomas Fuller by the indefatigable Londoner Walter White in his wide-ranging account of *A Month in Yorkshire* (1858). Superlatives seem unavoidable in any consideration of the largest of the English counties, whether relating to facts (the greatest number of abbeys, the highest waterfall) or to opinions (the finest cricketers, the strongest beer), and Wensleydale, too, requires them in full measure.

This rich dairy-farming country is the biggest of the dales, and the furthest from the surrounding industrial conurbations of Lancashire, southern Yorkshire and Teesside. 'It would be hard to imagine,' writes Peter Gunn, 'a more typically English landscape than these middle reaches of the Ure, as it flows past well wooded hills and fertile water-meadows. These are a perfect foil to those upland regions of high moors, mountainous tracts and beautiful intervening valleys.'

The Romans were here, and, later, the monks of Jervaulx and Fountains and the lesser abbey of Coverham. There are baronial castles at Middleham and Bolton, and the names of old feudal families (Scrope, Percy, Neville, Latimer) are

OVERLEAF
28 *Aysgarth Force in Wensleydale (sometimes known as Ure- or Yoredale), where the river Ure, tumbling over a series of falls, appears at its most turbulent and spectacular. Riverside walks are delightful in many parts of the Dales – here they are outstandingly dramatic.*

remembered in houses and churches. Ripon has one of the best of the smaller cathedrals, and a few miles from it is the superb 18th-century park of Studley Royal, a remarkable feat of imaginative landscaping set with jewels, as beautiful as the dale itself.

Aldborough   7 miles SE of Ripon, a gracious little brick-built village where the Romans had one of their more important fortresses. Its plan can be seen in a small museum on the site, which commands extensive views in all directions. Two mosaic pavements are well preserved (one is complete) in a field behind the museum – each about 10-foot square. 14th-century church, and a maypole on the green.

Askrigg   Once the market town of the upper dale (now superseded by Hawes); there were various small industries here such as brewing, cotton-spinning and knitting. Market cross with a stepped base, near the site of a former bullring. Pevsner considers the church the stateliest in the dale, and remarks on the beautiful vaulting of the tower and the powerful nave ceiling. Much of the Herriot television series was filmed here. Nappa Hall, a medieval fortified manor-house 1 mile E of the village is clearly to be seen across the valley from the main road S of the river; it has two castellated towers, one higher than the other. Geologists refer to the Askrigg Block or Massif, which comprises the carboniferous limestone and the Yoredale sandstones of the Craven district.

Aysgarth   Celebrated for a spectacular series of waterfalls (**28**) – half a mile of exciting riverside walk – painted by Turner. The Dales Park Centre (N of the river) is an invaluable source of general information. Predominantly 19th-century church; finely carved screen (*c*.1500) and reading desk presumed to have come from Jervaulx Abbey. Widened single-arch mid-16th-century bridge. The side valley of Bishopdale can be explored from Aysgarth, or from Wharfedale via Buckden.

Bainbridge   Beautiful village around a broad green, with the Bain Beck (England's shortest named river) cascading down from lovely Semer Water, one of the few natural lakes in Yorkshire. (Best views are from the Countersett side.)

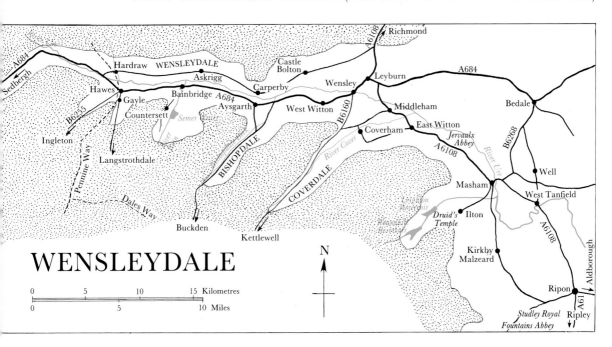

WENSLEYDALE

Ancient inn, the Rose and Crown (1443), houses the Bainbridge Horn, which was taken out and sounded at 9 o'clock every night from Holy-rood Day (late September) till Shrove Tuesday – a custom going back to the Middle Ages when it guided benighted travellers, though leaving them to fend for themselves on and after Ash Wednesday seems less charitable. In more recent centuries Bainbridge was a strong Quaker centre, as were Askrigg and Carperby (N of Aysgarth).

A Roman fort was established here from about AD 80, linked by road to Aldborough, Ribchester and Ilkley; the site is on private land E of the village, on top of a drumlin, one of the many little round-topped hills left by glacial action in this part of the dale.

Bolton Castle (30), in the village of Castle Bolton. Built by Richard Scrope, Lord Chancellor of England in the late 1300s. An almost picturebook example of what a castle should be, foursquare, of immense height, with towers at each corner and a central courtyard. Mary Queen of Scots was lodged here (1568–9), virtually a prisoner of Elizabeth I, whose protection she had sought after being forced to flee from Scotland. The stark stone staircase of the castle entrance is full of foreboding.

East Witton   Narrow 'estate' village on an elongated green, a charming prospect when approached from the east. Declined from its medieval status of market town (chartered 1306). Many houses rebuilt in the early 18th century by the Earl of Ailesbury, who owned the Jervaulx Abbey estate. Regency church (1809) noted for its good acoustics. The Ulshaw Bridge (1674) has massive cutwaters and, unusually, a sundial. Site of pre-Roman fort.

Fountains Abbey (31)   SW of Ripon, in the valley of the Skell, a tributary of the Ure. Since 1983 in the care of the National Trust, which has embarked on an extensive programme of building restoration and woodland management

29 *Fountains Hall (c. 1611) was built of stone taken from the abbey. Despite the elaborate façade and wide, mullioned windows, the impression is domestic and intimate compared with the grandeur of the neighbouring ruins.*

30 *Bolton castle, menacing and powerful as one approaches from the south. Built at the end of the 14th century, it commands a broad area of upper Wensleydale.*

(explained in detail in Fountains Hall (**29**), the house at the W end of the estate, at the entrance near the village of Sawley).

The abbey (1138–1247), magnificent relic of the greatest monastery in the north of England, and the most complete remains of a Cistercian abbey in the whole country, was built according to the standard pattern established by the Cistercian order in their foundation monastery at Clairvaux in France. Much here is unique in Europe as well – the imposing W range, for example (the first sight on entering through the gatehouse), almost entire and lit by 20 windows on the upper floor (the lay brothers' dormitory) over cellars and a refectory. The great Perpendicular church tower was built to the orders of the last abbot, Marmaduke Huby (elected 1495).

The first monks called it Fountains from the number of springs they found here. They came in 1132 from the Benedictine abbey in York, which had become more comfortable and worldly than they considered proper. The austerity they desired was not hard to find for the valley was thick with thornbushes, and more suitable for wild animals than human beings. They spent the first winter sheltering under rocks, and later under a tree, living on bread supplied by a sympathetic archbishop. Soon a chapel was built, and land cleared for a garden, and the little community was taken into the Cistercian order, which had already founded a house at Rievaulx. Gradually endowments accrued, and valuable grants of land, eventually forming the basis of incomparable wealth (see p.4). Besides their vast and pioneering industry in wool production and trade, the monks carried on lead- and coal-mining and iron-smelting enterprises, sea and river fishing, and fish farming in artificial lakes created close to the abbey.

The present appearance of the site is due in great measure to the Aislabies, father

41

and son, who incorporated it into the Studley Royal estate in 1768, clearing the ground and setting the buildings in a sweeping expanse of green. A small museum near the gatehouse provides information about the abbey buildings, and contains two items of note: a curious acoustic jar, a large, rather crude pottery object, one of many which were placed under the floor of the choir stalls to add resonance to the singing; and fragments of carved corbels in the so-called Nidderdale marble, a warm, mauvish, pearly stone which enriched the interior of the church (see p.46).

Peter Gunn, in his invaluable book on the Dales, notes the peculiar good fortune of the local stone, 'the palest of greys, but warm, responsive to the light, intensely living' – only a few miles away it would have been gritstone, which blackens dispiritingly as it weathers. 'The beauty of the architecture', he writes, 'is perhaps best seen from the east, where the glorious Chapel of the Nine Altars, with its Early English lancet windows flanking the great Perpendicular east window, is reflected in the still waters of the Skell. Here can be appreciated to the full the crispness, the freshness, the sober delicacy of the Cistercian style of monastic building – something very near perfection.'

Hawes Tough little town at the head of the dale, whose busy narrow streets have the appearance of having grown up haphazardly, like those of its one-time rival, the adjacent village of Gayle, a more ancient Celtic settlement. Good centre for tourists, especially walkers (it is on the Pennine Way). Highest market town in Yorkshire (800 feet) and second highest in England (after Alston, 1000 feet). The famous Wensleydale cheese is manufactured here. The Upper Dales Folk Museum is excellent: imaginatively displayed, this great collection has been made over many years by Joan Ingilby and Marie Hartley, authors of many good books on the Yorkshire scene.

Two miles N is the dramatic Hardraw Force *(title page)*, where it is possible to walk right behind the waterfall. It has always been a popular place, especially in the years immediatley following the arrival of the railway to Hawes in 1877, when visitors came in their hundreds for the brass band and choral contests which were regular events in the amphitheatre of the Hardraw ravine.

Jervaulx Abbey (32) Close to the road between Masham and Middleham. Like Fountains, a Cistercian foundation of the mid-12th century, though smaller. It is a romantic ruin clothed in wild flowers. The last abbot was beheaded at Tyburn for his alleged part in the Pilgrimage of Grace (1536, see p.5), after which considerable destruction was visited upon the abbey.

Masham Locally pronounced Mass'm. Chartered in 1250 for a market which continued to the end of the 19th century. Traction Engine Rally and Steam Fair every July. Noted for brewing since 1827 – one specially strong ale is called Old Peculier, and nicknamed 'lunatic broth'. 9th-century Saxon cross in the churchyard. Druid's Temple **(33)**, 5 miles SW, near Ilton.

Middleham Unassuming, dignified village whose importance now lies in the rearing of racehorses, made possible by the wide open spaces of this part of the dale. Georgian houses and grey stone cottages shelter under startlingly impressive walls of a castle whose splendour has fallen from a time of unassailable power. Strategically placed to guard Coverdale and the route from Skipton to Richmond, the castle is of Norman origin, with one of the largest keeps in England. In the mid-15th century it was the virtual capital of the north of England, and the seat of the immensely strong arch-fixer Richard Neville, Earl of Warwick (known as the Kingmaker; died 1471). In 1469 he had Edward IV imprisoned here, and in previous years he had charge of the upbringing of Prince Richard of Gloucester, who returned here to live as lord of the north, notably wise and widely respected, until he attained the throne as Richard III. His death at Bosworth in 1485 brought

31 *The magnificent ruins of Fountains Abbey evoke the splendour of medieval monastic architecture more completely than anything else in England. The church's great tower, 170 feet high, is a 16th-century addition to the 12th- and 13th-century buildings. The living quarters were built over the River Skell, visible in the foreground; it was customary for monasteries to be built near running water, which provided drainage.*

an end to the Wars of the Roses, and the decline of the castle dates from this time. Its final ruin came with the removal of its roof, ordered after the Civil War (mid-17th century); many of the village houses were built of stone taken from the castle. The view from the south gives an impression of the medieval might of Middleham.

Coverdale is one of the bigger side valleys of the Ure. Here are the sparse remains of early-13th-century Coverham Abbey, now on private land. The scholar–priest Miles Coverdale (1488–1568) is presumed to have been born in this valley, and he made the name famous: the Coverdale Bible (1535, 1539) was the first complete English translation. His versions of the Psalms are still in use in the Book of Common Prayer.

Ripon Smallest city in Yorkshire, and one of the oldest boroughs in England. It is claimed to have been chartered in 886 by Alfred the Great, who presented a horn to the Wakeman (or Watchman, later the Mayor); there is currently some acrimonious local controversy about this – fact or legend? Whatever the truth of the matter, the custom is kept of sounding a horn every evening in the market square. The original horn may be seen in the Town Hall, which bears a motto from Psalm 127: 'Except ye Lord keep ye Cittie, ye Wakeman waketh in vain'. The Wakeman's House, in the market square, is timber-framed, whereas most of Ripon is brick, resembling places further E rather than characteristically Dales. It has a much-favoured racecourse, 1 mile SE, from which there is one of the finest views of the compact city and its cathedral.

St Wilfrid (634–709) founded an abbey here and dedicated its church to St Peter in 672; the cathedral is thus one of the oldest ecclesiastical foundations in the country. Wilfrid's name was added to the dedication after his death. This dynamic

32 *Jervaulx Abbey, part of a private estate but open to visitors. It is a romantic ruin, well kept but less manicured than many such places, in a gentle valley. The name means Ure (Jer = Yore) Vale.*

33 *Druid's Temple at Ilton, near Masham, a most delicious folly of the Regency period (c. 1830). It is a replica of Stonehenge, and is now hidden in Forestry Commission woodland – a short walk well worth taking in this secluded part of lower Wensleydale.*

Northumbrian priest succeeded in bringing the disparate northern churches into line with Roman practice at the Synod of Whitby (663). He travelled three times to Rome, reputedly walking all the way at the age of 70, and brought back to Ripon holy relics which were displayed in the crypt (now the Treasury). His church was destroyed by the Danes in the 10th century. The greater part of the cathedral which replaced it 200 years later is the work of Archbishop Roger Pont l'Eveque, and is a splendid example of Norman Transitional building (round arches giving way to pointed). The Early English W front (**35**) belongs to the first part of the 13th century, and following years brought work and embellishment of an equally high order, e.g. the E window, the carved bosses of the chancel ceiling, the choir stalls and misericords, and the Lady chapel. Some indifferent modern work has done nothing to detract from the essential homogeneity of this beautiful medieval cathedral.

Just 3 miles SE of Ripon is Newby Hall, a mellow red-brick stately home in the classical late-17th-century style of Wren. Later additions by the great Yorkshire architect John Carr; superb Adam interiors and Gobelin tapestries. 25 acres of beautifully planned gardens alongside a lovely stretch of the river Ure. Church by William Burges (see below).

Studley Royal John Aislabie was Chancellor of the Exchequer in 1720, when his public career was abruptly concluded by the South Sea Bubble disaster, a reckless speculation which led to the ruin of thousands and the collapse of the government. Aislabie retired to Studley to devote the rest of his life to the creation of this remarkable park. The river Skell was canalised to run in the middle of the valley, with cascades, ponds and a lake; bridges, clipped hedges and grassy embankments provided delicious vistas. His son William continued the work and incorporated Fountains Abbey into the estate (every 18th-century gentleman's park required a ruin – here he could surpass all others). The great house, built some way from the valley, on the N side of the park, was destroyed by fire this century. A number of buildings remain, all in the elegant taste of the mid-1700s: classical temples, a gothic octagonal tower, a banqueting house, and stables in Palladian style. Although the ostensible purpose was solely to give pleasure, the Aislabies did not escape criticism. Benjamin Newton (1762–1830) objected to 'the silly improvement and moderning of the ground which Fountains and many others exhibit', and 'the display of Grecian building which shews more the wealth than the taste of the proprietor'.

At the W end of the main avenue is St Mary's church (1870s), considered to be the masterpiece of the individual, not to say eccentric, architect William Burges. Its outward appearance is chilly Victorian gothic, but inside is an attractive mix of the meticulous and the exuberant, translating into real terms the medieval trappings of the pre-Raphaelite dream. The main body of the church is restrained, the grey columns enriched with blue marble shafts. Was Burges echoing the blue Nidderdale marble once used in the abbey? The chancel is a veritable riot of colour, blue ceiling panels overlaid with gold stars, and a lovely abundance of gilding and scarlet; the stained glass is bright, clear colour, and the figures have cheerful innocent pink faces, quite unlike the usual sickly greenness of the period. Although it was constructed principally as a mausoleum, the church (open for viewing during the summer) reflects the pure pleasure principle which is now the most striking quality of the Studley Royal estate.

Wensley, once the main centre of the dale, has given place to Leyburn, possibly owing to depopulation by a severe outbreak of plague in the mid-16th century. Four-arched, 15th-century bridge, one of the most beautiful in the Dales. Lovely

34 *Holy Trinity church, Wensley, is richly furnished with monuments and carvings such as this charming 17th-century bench end. The great northern baronial family of Scrope were patrons of the church.*

35 *William Aislabie planted fine avenues of trees in Studley Royal Park. This north-eastern one, the grandest, is aligned on the imposing west front of Ripon cathedral.*

church (1245; **34**) contains Anglo-Saxon fragments, memorials to the Scrope family (including a brass of 1360s), wall painting (*c.* 1330) representing the Quick and the Dead, finely carved screen possibly brought from Easby, and an 18th-century two-decker pulpit and box pews with matching decoration.

West Tanfield The first big village at the E end of the dale, where a handsome Georgian three-arched bridge crosses the Ure running NE before turning towards Ripon. Right beside the river is the battlemented Marmion Tower, a gatehouse, all that remains of the castle of the Marmions, who have entirely disappeared, apart from their crumbling monuments in the church beside the tower. The church is 12th-14th century, but considerably restored; pieces of Anglo-Saxon stone carving, and some fragments of medieval stained glass in a window in the N aisle.

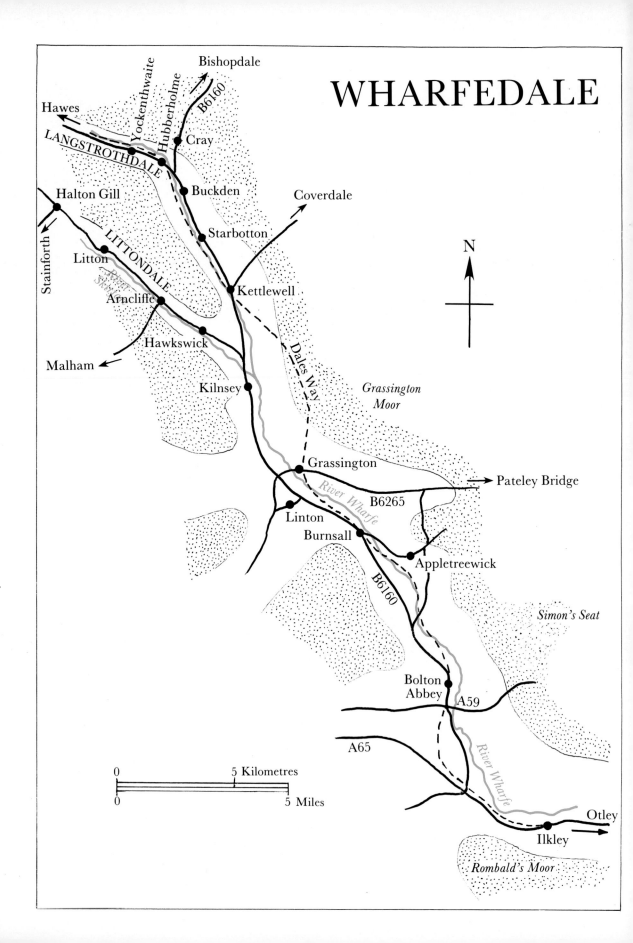

WHARFEDALE

Wharfedale

Wharfedale has at its centre one of the finest sights in all Yorkshire – Bolton Abbey(**36**), rich in romance and history, and recorded by painters and writers throughout the centuries. In *Modern Painters*, Ruskin described 'the river, whose clear brown water, stealing first into mere threads between the separate pebbles of shingle, and eddying in soft golden lines towards its central current, flows out of amber into ebony, and glides calm and deep below the rock on the opposite shore.' With a glance upstream towards the remembered and dreaded chasm, the Strid, and around at meadow and moorland, he is seized by 'an instinctive apprehension of the strength and greatness of the wild northern land. It is to the association of this power and border sternness with the sweet peace and tender decay of Bolton Priory that the scene owes its distinctive charm.'

Below Bolton the road runs between hedgerows vivid in summer with dog roses, blue cranesbill, angelica and meadowsweet, to more open pastoral country between Ilkley and Harewood, and the charming tributary valley of Washburndale (see map on p.17). At Grassington and thereafter it is limestone, brilliant emerald and white, hillsides naturally terraced, and high up are botanically rich limestone pavements where Richard Mabey found rock roses growing so densely that their pollen scented the wind. Old villages and old walls (extra high in places where enclosures had to keep in horses as well as sheep) are scattered along the dale, and the surrounding hills press together the winding river and its adjacent road. Just north of the mighty lowering crag at Kilnsey, the road forks into the

37 *Barden Bridge is thought to have been built at the command of Lady Anne Clifford, c. 1659. At one time this was a busy route – the main thoroughfare between Skipton and Pateley Bridge. At the end of the 1920s the bridge was partially dismantled, strengthened and painstakingly reconstructed.*

38 *The Strid. This sinister and deceptive chasm has claimed the lives of many who have been tempted to jump across. What was once a waterfall has merged with underground courses of varying and treacherous depth, only recently and only partially explored.*

delightful diversion of Littondale, and leads to dramatic routes 'over the tops' into Airedale and Ribblesdale.

Appletreewick   Locally pronounced Abtrick. Hillside village between Burnsall and Bolton, from which there are magnificent views of the valley. The Roman road from Ilkley to Bainbridge passed this way; 3rd-century artifacts have been discovered in the area. Sites of lead mines between here and Grassington. This part of Wharfedale saw prolonged and sometimes bloody quarrels and lawsuits amongst the feudal landowners, mainly on account of hunting rights; by the end of the Stuart period the deer had virtually disappeared.

Arncliffe see **Littondale**

Bolton Abbey (36)   An Augustinian priory (never an abbey), founded in 1151. Most of the surviving buildings are 13th century. The tower, started in 1520, was still uncompleted by the Dissolution (1539). The ruins owe their fame to the outstandingly picturesque site, a gently sloping grassy bank embraced in a sweeping curve of the river, very shallow here, overshadowed by dark cliffs and hanging woods on the further side. A footbridge and stepping stones lead across to a point for the best of all views of the abbey.

Lady Alicia de Romilly, of the Norman family which occupied Skipton castle (see p.13), founded the abbey in memory of her son the 'Boy of Egremont', who was drowned in the Strid (**38**), a sinister chasm a mile or so upstream. It is the apparent narrowness of the space between the rocks above the torrent which has tempted so many, through the centuries, to try jumping over the deceptively wide gap. In Trollope's *Lady Anna* (1874), all the members of a picnic party manage the jump, although the heroine sprains her ankle – altogether a thoroughly bad example.

39 Burnsall, one of Wharfedale's loveliest villages. The handsome bridge was re-erected in 1884 after severe flooding in the previous year. St Wilfrid's church, in the centre of the picture, is mainly Perpendicular, and like so many in these parts contains fragments of Anglo-Saxon carvings.

Priory and estates soon passed from the Romillys to the great northern family of Clifford, who ruled these parts from the early years of the 14th century and owned the impressive Barden Tower (upstream again). The fiercest of them, Lord John 'the Butcher' Clifford, was arraigned for treason after the Battle of Wakefield (1460), and forced to forfeit part of his estates; his son was brought up in hiding among shepherds, and was afterwards known as the Shepherd Lord. He lived most of his life quietly at Barden, studying with the monks of the abbey. Much loved, he had no trouble in raising a force which he led, at the age of 60, in support of the King's army against the Scots at Flodden (1513). He rebuilt Barden Tower some time after 1485. It was again reconstructed by his descendant Lady Anne Clifford (see Skipton) during the 1650s.

The Bolton estate descended to the Dukes of Devonshire, and the priory gatehouse has been incorporated into Bolton Hall, the house on the W side of the church. The W end of the abbey church is currently used by the parish, and the tower is being rebuilt.

Buckden   Centre of a deer forest in feudal times, as its name indicates. Situated on a steep hillside above the river and below Buckden Pike (2302 feet). The dale forks here, the main road going up Bishopdale via Kidstones Pass, past the hamlet and waterfalls of Cray, and over into Wensleydale; a lesser road goes into Langstrothdale. Excellent walking centre.

Burnsall (**39**)   An especially captivating sight from the road coming up from Bolton. St Wilfrid's church, mainly Perpendicular, has Anglo-Saxon fragments of carved stone, two 'hog-back' tombstones, and a Norman font. After Burnsall, hedges give way to limestone walling.

Farnley see **Washburndale**

40 *Wharfedale between Burnsall and Barden.*

Grassington   Cobbled, irregular market place and intriguing alleys leading from it make this an exceptionally pretty village. Medieval (widened) four-arched bridge. Hall of 13th-century origin. The town has flourished as a tourist centre ever since the opening of the railway from Skipton in 1902. The regular service was closed in 1930, but excursions were continued for some years after. Folk Museum (**43**) and National Park Information Centre.

On Grassington Moor, to the N towards Hebden, much evidence of lead workings, going back to Roman times, but at their peak in the 18th and 19th centuries (see Swaledale).

Hubberholme   Name thought to derive from that of a 9th-century Viking chieftain, Hubba. Characteristic small grey Dales church, with a low, square tower, rather rugged inside, and a rood loft (1558; **41**) rarely found in England. Two of its curates are commemorated: Thomas Lindley, who until the age of 80 used to ride on horseback from his home in Halton Gill to take services here; and Miles Wilson, curate in 1743, who wrote perhaps the first space-age novel (with the purpose of teaching astronomy), about a man going to the moon from the top of Pen-y-ghent.

Ilkley   The *-ley* suffix denotes a woodland clearing, and marks the progress of Anglo-Saxon settlers making their way W into the then inhospitable, densely forested Dales. Anglo-Saxon crosses in the church (**42**). A museum in the old manor-house next door has Bronze-Age carvings collected on the moors, many showing the concentric incised circles and rounded depressions of the mysterious 'cup and ring' motif. Rombald's Moor, to the S and W, is rich in ancient earthworks; a stone circle is known as the Twelve Apostles. In Roman times Ilkley was *Olicana*, a fort on the road between Manchester and Aldborough.

41 *St Michael's church, Hubberholme, has the only surviving rood loft in western Yorkshire. It is dated 1558 and was designed as a gallery for singers.*

42 *These three well-preserved Anglo-Saxon crosses originally stood in the churchyard of All Saints, Ilkley. They have recently been re-erected inside the church.*

The discovery of medicinal waters brought prosperity to 'the Malvern of the north' in the 19th century, though not on the scale of Harrogate. Ever since, it has been a favoured residential area for Leeds and Bradford, its self-satisfied air somewhat at variance with the black humour and nonsense refrain of the raucous popular folk song *Ilkley Moor Ba't'at* (*ba't'at* = 'without a hat'). At Guiseley, 4 miles SE, is the splendid Harry Ramsden's, which claims to be the biggest fish and chip shop in the world.

Kettlewell Once as busy as Grassington is now – market, corn mill, lead mines and smelting. It stands at the junction with the road to Coverdale, and belonged to the monks of Coverham. The dale is very shaggy here; traces of ancient field systems (lynchets) can be traced on the hillsides. Kettlewell and Starbotton are excellent starting points for numerous good walks, such as the riverside path updale to Buckden, or fell walks to Great Whernside, Cam Head or Buckden Pike.

Kilnsey takes its name from the lime kilns which were once a ubiquitous feature of this part of the dale, when lime for use in building and as a fertilizer was worked in small kilns whose circular remains may still be found, although their glowing fires no longer dot the hillsides.

The crag is a startling feature (**45**), brooding over the road across a stream bright with golden mimulus (only one indication of the botanist's paradise in these parts), and contrasts starkly with the wide, flat meadows at its foot, formed by a post-glacial lake. Kilnsey was an important outpost of the Fountains Abbey complex, and still holds an annual show.

43 *Cottages converted for use as a Folk Museum in the large and attractive village of Grassington, in the middle of Wharfedale.*

Langstrothdale The head of Wharfedale; the river rises in Green Field and Oughtershaw Becks. It comprises the hamlets of Raisgill (with a packhorse bridge), Yockenthwaite, Deepdale and Oughtershaw, and last and most remote

44 *About half a mile from the village of Linton, close beside the Wharfe, is the parish church – originally late 12th century though largely rebuilt in the 15th century. Its modest exterior conceals a very fine interior, in parts Norman, Early English and Perpendicular. The carved wooden bosses in the chancel roof are primitive, almost pagan.*

Cam Houses (which actually belongs to the township of Horton-in-Ribblesdale), where the Pennine Way and the Dales Way meet. Spectacular drive over Oughtershaw Side and through Sleddale into Hawes.

Linton One of the most attractive villages of this dale which has so many. Running through the village green is a beck crossed in five separate ways – clapper, packhorse and motor-road bridges, stepping stones and a ford. The 17th-century Hall faces the green, and opposite, Fountains Hospital (almshouses, 1720s), grandiose and ornate, with Venetian windows and nothing of indigenous character. Church in a delightfully pastoral setting (**44**), some way from the village centre.

Littondale The river Skirfare (**46**) flows through this lovely side valley to join the Wharfe above Kilnsey. Particular interest for anglers, botanists and geologists; there is also hang-gliding at Knipe Scar, near Hawkswick. Cuckoos and curlews sing till near midnight in midsummer. The name of the biggest village, Arncliffe, is said to mean the eagle's cliff, though there is some dispute. It is the starting point of several breath-taking walks as well as an exhilarating drive over into Malham or Stainforth.

Otley Workaday small town in the lower dale, of some historical interest and worth exploring. Medieval bridge and large church with important fragments of Anglo-Saxon crosses. Unique monument in the churchyard: a railway tunnel entrance, a memorial to the workers who died during the construction of the Bramhope tunnel on the Leeds–Thirsk railway, 1845–9. Otley was the birthplace of the great cabinet-maker Thomas Chippendale (1718–79).

45 *Kilnsey Crag rears ominously over the road going westwards up Wharfedale, its ruggedness a sharp contrast with the lush green of the wide, flat meadows at its foot.*

46 *The bridge at Arncliffe in Littondale (a side valley of Wharfedale), whose river Skirfare runs through some of the most delectable of Dales scenery. Clear traces of ancient Celtic field enclosures may be seen south of the village.*

Washburndale (see map on p.17) The river Washburn rises on Pock Stones Moor E of Appletreewick, and runs into the Wharfe at Pool, between Otley and Harewood. A relatively unfrequented valley in rolling country, well wooded and watered, with a network of winding lanes and footpaths. Four reservoirs, softened by typical conifer plantations, have become naturalised, and there is sailing on Thruscross, the highest of them. 17th- and 18th-century stone-built houses in villages such as Leathley, Fewston, Timble, Blubberhouses.

The great house of Farnley Hall (not on public view) was originally Elizabethan, and is important for having a 1790 addition by Yorkshire architect John Carr, considered to be his masterpiece. Turner made the house his headquarters for his many visits to Yorkshire, and it has a great collection of his paintings. The notorious folk villain Guy Fawkes, one of the perpetrators of the Gunpowder Plot (1605), belonged to the Fawkes family of Farnley Hall, who still live there.

47 *The river Wharfe near Kettlewell in the early evening.*

Calderdale and Brontë Country

See map on following page

> Where the millstone of sky
> Grinds light and shadow so purple-fine

Our Yorkshire-born Poet Laureate, Ted Hughes, captures in his poem cycle *Remains of Elmet* the contrasting elements of this region in lines reverberant with the ancient geology and endless human struggle that have made it unique and set it apart from the rest of Britain. It is bounded to the north by the inhospitable mass of Rombald's Moor, rich in prehistoric remains (see p.53), between the rivers Wharfe and Aire, and to the south by the equally formidable Blackstone Edge – the Andes of England, Defoe called it (*A Tour of the Whole Island of Great Britain*, 1724–6). The middle Aire flows south-east from Skipton; the Calder rises on the Lancashire border, is joined by the Ryburn at Sowerby Bridge and passes south of Halifax, eventually to join the Aire at Castleford and run into the Ouse and the Humber estuary.

Until recent times the riversides were densely wooded, and in many places remain so. In a deep glen of surpassing secret beauty below Cunning Corner (by Rishworth), or in the lovely National Trust lands of Hardcastle Crags (north of Hebden Bridge), it is easy to imagine yourself 100 miles from an industrial town instead of a mere 8 or 10. The dark peat of the moors has never succumbed to cultivation, so that farms and old settlements are mostly found along a band midway between river and moor. The townships (or 'towns' as they are usually called, for 'village' is a term seldom used) were sparse and scattered, and to come from as many as 6 miles away was to be a stranger. There is a singular wild outlandishness about many place-names – Krumlin, Scammonden, Outlane, Catherine Slack, Flints.

Haworth, on the other hand, is almost too famous, rivalling Stratford-upon-Avon as the most visited literary shrine in the country. The church dominates the top of the old village, as do other churches in this area, such as Heptonstall (**54**). Anyone seeking authentic atmosphere must tramp over timeless moorland, or stroll through less frequented Calderdale villages which still retain some air of what Haworth must have been in the Brontës' day. Near a solitary hilltop farm we may, with Emily Brontë, 'guess the power of the north wind blowing over the edge by the excessive slant of a few stunted firs at the end of the house, and by a range of gaunt thorns all stretching their limbs one way, as if craving alms of the sun'. And we may experience for ourselves what 'wuthering' is: 'a significant local adjective,' Emily writes, 'descriptive of the atmospheric tumult to which [the house] is exposed in stormy weather.' (*Wuthering Heights*, Ch.1.)

Although the Brontës were writing during the 1830s and 1840s, some of their

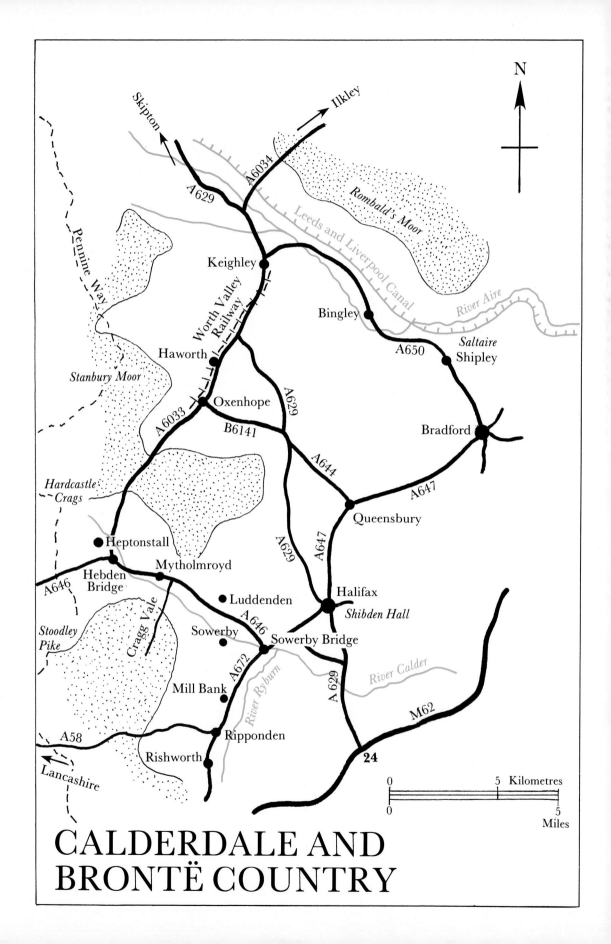

CALDERDALE AND
BRONTË COUNTRY

48 Sowerby (pronounced Sorby) is remarkable for its handsome classical St Peter's church (1763–6), with galleries, Corinthian columns and rounded apse, following the style of Holy Trinity, Leeds. Both churches show the influence of James Gibbs, who designed the Radcliffe Camera, Oxford, and the Senate House, Cambridge. The most distinguished son of the village, John Tillotson (1630–94), is commemorated with a statue in the church. Born at Haugh End, Sowerby, he became one of England's most famous preachers, and was created Archbishop of Canterbury in 1691.

stories have an earlier setting, looking back several decades to a rural way of life when the industrial revolution was in its infancy. Throughout the 18th century the woollen industry was growing rapidly, with watermills turning in the valleys, and an inexorable quickening of pace as technology advanced. Such inventions as the Flying Shuttle (1738) and the Spinning Jenny (1764) enabled the output of a single worker to be increased many times over. The dual economy of previous centuries gradually disappeared as factories took over home-based work. No longer could members of a family be both farmers and wool workers (spinning or weaving) according to the needs of moment and weather. Nevertheless the characteristic stone-built weavers' cottages of the 17th and early 18th centuries, lit by a long range of first-floor windows, are a constant reminder of pre-industrial work patterns.

The magnificent Piece Hall (**51**) in Halifax is an eloquent monument to the town's predominance in the highly organised wool and worsted trade of this period. Fleeces were collected and combed, and sent by packhorse far afield into Craven and the Dales, where milestones measured the distance not to London but to Halifax; the wool was spun and then woven at home, four spinners supplying one weaver, and then returned to the Piece Hall for sale and eventual export. A 'piece' was 38 yards long and its weaving might have taken above two weeks.

The 19th century brought dramatic change to what Charlotte Brontë, in her preface to *Wuthering Heights*, described as a 'remote and unclaimed region', by-passed by history, too forbidding even for the monks of the Middle Ages, too poor and off the beaten track to interest the feudal barons. The prosperity of the wool trade came about because of water. In a land of hard rock, steep gradients and

thin soil the water runs off plentifully, not absorbed as in the softer limestone further north:

> Millstone-grit – a soul-grinding sandstone. . .
> A people converting their stony ideas
> To woollen weave, thick worsteds, dense fustians

Ted Hughes, Remains of Elmet

The gathering speed of change reached breakneck pace with the substitution of steam for water power, and an extensive network of canals brought coal to mills which no longer needed to be close to a river. In her novel *Shirley* (1849), Charlotte Brontë drew on local experience to treat the perennial issue of new technology, which led to the bitter Luddite riots of 1812, when workers smashed the machines they feared would put an end to their livelihood. In 1813 at least 30 men from these parts were hanged in York, and many more were imprisoned. Three times the military were brought to Halifax – in 1826 to protect the power looms, in 1839 against the Chartists, and to quell further industrial trouble in 1842. Meantime Halifax was overtaken as the wool and worsted centre of the country by Bradford, whose population increased from 6000 in 1800 to 42,000 by 1848. The impressive mill at Saltaire (now a conservation area), employing over 3000, was one of many, but differed from the rest in having a model village (see pp.70–1).

With the almost complete demise of the woollen industry in the past 30 years, and the near total disappearance of the great mills, life and landscape have again been transformed. Smoke emission was banned by act of parliament after World War II, so that statutory clean air has effected a quiet but profound revolution, optimistic (gardens flourish as never before), health-giving and labour-saving

49 *The churchyard at Haworth, with the Brontë Parsonage in the background. The gabled end of the house was added after the Brontës' time, and together with the original rooms is now a museum.*

(daily washing of steps, pavement and windows is no longer necessary). There is now a certain wry irony in the once-familiar local saying, 'Where there's muck there's brass.'

In her journal (1836) Charlotte Brontë described the view from Crimsworth Dean, north of Hebden Bridge: 'Huddersfield and the hills beyond it were all veiled in blue mist, the woods of Hepton and Heaton Lodge were clouding the water edge, and the Calder, silent but bright, was shooting among them like a silver arrow.' Many such incomparable prospects are to be had at high points along the 50 miles of the spectacular Calderdale Way, ridge upon ridge of blue and purple moorland, given a particular character and flavour by the close proximity of busy towns and old industry.

Cragg Vale   Secluded valley S of Mytholmroyd, notorious in the mid-18th century for forgery. The 'Cragg Vale Coiners' found it easy to clip the undifferentiated, unmilled gold coins then current, and to recast the clippings. Around 1760 there were thought to be as many as 70 men of this valley in the gang. The ringleaders were eventually hanged or imprisoned. Relics of the coiners in the Grammar School Museum, Heptonstall. David Hartley, the 'King of the coiners', is buried in the old churchyard here.

Halifax   The name is said to mean 'Holy Face'. A legend whose origin is lost in the mists of time tells that a portion of the face (or perhaps a death mask?) of St John the Baptist was preserved here as a holy relic. The face appears on the town's coat of arms, which adorns the splendid painted iron gates of the Piece Hall (50). This cloth market and exchange was built in the 1770s on an unusually grand scale – a vast open rectangle on sloping ground, arcaded galleries along its four

50 *A detail of the ornate, painted iron gates at the south entrance to the Piece Hall, Halifax, which replaced the original oak door in 1871. They are decorated with the town's coat of arms, the emblem of the Holy Face, and a Latin inscription meaning 'Unless the Lord keep the City [they labour in vain that build it]'.*

sides, two storeys on the upper side and three on the lower, containing over 300 rooms. More like Italy than Yorkshire. There are no other remaining cloth markets and none was comparable. It was restored in the 1970s and now houses shops, a museum and a tourist centre, and markets and concerts in the courtyard.

Beyond the lower (E) side of the Piece Hall stands the parish church of St John, one of the largest parish churches in West Yorkshire. The smoke-blackened exterior belies, at first glance, its fine Perpendicular quality. It is unusual in having a clerestory in the chancel but not in the nave. Curious gargoyles. Inside, beautiful 17th-century wooden ceilings, and carvings on the chancel stalls. The nearby free-standing cleaned spire is all that remains of the United Reformed church recently destroyed by fire. Towards the town centre, the busy covered market (1895) is well worth a visit; it has a cast-iron and glass roof, and attractive central clock.

A ten-minute walk across town from the Piece Hall leads to the Gibbet, a replica of the guillotine used on anyone caught stealing as little as 13 pence, which gave rise to the so-called 'Thieves Litany': 'From Hell, Hull and Halifax Good Lord deliver us.' (Hull was where men could be pressganged aboard ship.) The original gibbet blade, used from the 13th century until the last execution in 1650 when it was banned by Cromwell, is displayed in the Piece Hall Pre-industrial Museum.

The Town Hall was designed (*c.* 1860) by Sir Charles Barry, architect of the Houses of Parliament, to 'serve as an exponent of the life and soul of the City'. Competing claimants to such a title might well be the great Crossley's Mills, Dean Clough, which fill a vast area at the lowest point of the town, alongside the Keighley road. No longer working, it is almost the last survivor of many scores of such mills which dominated the scene until the 1930s, and produced the wealth and the misery of the last century. The striking landmark of Wainhouse Tower (on Skircoat Moor Road, towards Sowerby Bridge) combines practicality (albeit unrealised – it was never used as a chimney) with lavish ornament, and for good measure an eccentric story. Mr Wainhouse is said to have built it so high – 253 feet – in order to see into his neighbour's garden. A chimney surrounded by a spiral staircase and an outer octagonal casing is topped by a corona of fantastic Italianate or oriental design, with a viewing platform, occasionally open to the public, 369 steps up from the base.

Pevsner's description of the Town Hall, 'a monument of self-confident High Victorianism', applies equally strongly to Bankfield House (on the road to Queensbury), built by Edward Akroyd, one of the wealthiest mill owners and an M.P. 1857–9 and (for Halifax) 1865–74. A palatial portico gives directly on to a magnificent staircase with Italianate wall painting of considerable elegance, leading up to inlaid floors and ornate fireplaces in the *piano nobile*. The house is now the Bankfield Museum, containing among its treasures exhibits of toys, relics domestic and regimental, and a small collection of modern paintings. Akroyd was an energetic philanthropist, founder of the Yorkshire Penny Bank (to educate the poor in Thrift), and of the Akroyden Estate – 350 houses plus a central park and allotments, Halifax's version of Saltaire.

Beacon Hill, the highest of the sheltering hills to the E, is one in the chain with Almondbury and Blackstone Edge on which beacons were lit to spread news (e.g. the defeat of the Spanish Armada in 1588). Close by, about 1 mile from the town centre, is Shibden Hall, a fine early-15th-century house set in 83 acres of park and excellently preserved as a museum. It has plain half-timbers, stone additions and a little tower; the stable yard contains a folk museum, and in front a terraced garden overlooks a lake and woodland. Inside, the collection of household furniture of various periods, including much oak, 'country Chippendale', tester beds, dressers

51 The Piece Hall, Halifax, dates from the 1770s. It was the foremost clothmarket and exchange in the north of England. There are more than 300 rooms along its arcaded galleries. In the past two decades it has been magnificently restored. The spire is all that remains of the former United Reformed church.

etc., and an untidy Victorian nursery, is presented to look as though the family has just gone out. A lively former owner, Anne Lister, member of a prominent local family, was responsible for the later (1830s) remodelling of the house and creation of the lake, and left her own graphic accounts of local history in the distressful years of the early 19th century.

52 *Landscape with mill buildings between Haworth and Oxenhope.*

Perhaps the most remarkable and unexpected of Halifax's contributions to human well-being was the invention of cat's eyes, the glass studs set in self-cleaning rubber pads now found on roads all over the world. Percy Shaw (1890–1976) told how he first had the idea from catching the reflection of a cat's eyes in his headlights when driving across the moors on a dark winter's night. His invention was patented in 1934, but only took off after 1945. Almost a recluse, he lived modestly in Boothtown, Halifax, and at his death was reputed to be worth £17 million.

Haworth   Now a spreading, dark West Yorkshire town, much grown from the hilltop village to which the Reverend Patrick Brontë brought his family in 1820. The main street, still paved with stone setts and closed to motor traffic, leads to the Brontë home at the Parsonage (**49**). This modest, foursquare house, where Mr Brontë refused to have curtains for fear of fire, and where the old Aunt Branwell clattered about on pattens for fear of the damp stone floors, was enlarged towards the road by a later incumbent, and has been a museum since 1928. It faces the church (rebuilt 1880 – only plaques mark the Brontë tombs) across a graveyard rather gloomier now than in the Brontës' time, when there were no upright tombstones or dreary sycamores. It is almost impossible to realise anything of the solitude and passionate intensity of these writers' lives, by turns so sorrowful and so ecstatic, in present-day Haworth.

Much has been made of identifying houses described in the novels – they are even signposted from Haworth – but scholars agree that there can be no single, exact location. Top Withens, the ruined farmhouse on Stanbury Moor, 4 miles SW of Haworth, is much visited for its popular association with Emily's great novel *Wuthering Heights*. The house in the book, which had 'grotesque carving . . . a wilderness of crumbling griffins, and shameless little boys', was larger and more decorated, and may have been based on the now demolished High Sunderland Hall, near Halifax.

Wycoller Hall, near Colne, over the border in Lancashire, is traditionally the site of Ferndean Manor in Charlotte Brontë's *Jane Eyre*. The resemblance is sketchy, but Wycoller is a place to be seen for itself, a romantic and, until recently, totally deserted village (deserted since the introduction of power looms and the move towards manufacturing in the towns) in a charming moorland hollow, with a newly created country park nearby. Ancient clam bridge, possibly Iron Age.

The Worth Valley steam railway is of nostalgic interest for all train lovers. It runs from Keighley to Oxenhope, and has a station at Haworth. The railway was an ordinary commercial one from 1867 to 1962; on its demise a group of enthusiasts formed a preservation society so successfully that the line was re-opened in 1968, to be managed as a private railway, very much a working museum. A remarkable number of old steam engines has been collected and can be seen at Haworth and Oxenhope stations.

Hebden Bridge (55)   Picturesque mill town dating from the late 18th century, when it superseded Heptonstall with the advent of the Rochdale Canal (1790s). Its particular attraction owes much to the constricted site which forced high building – there are many four-storey houses with galleries giving access to separate dwellings in the upper portions. Wainwright in his Pennine Way guide found crossing this

53 *The former village school in Haworth, where Charlotte Brontë taught.*

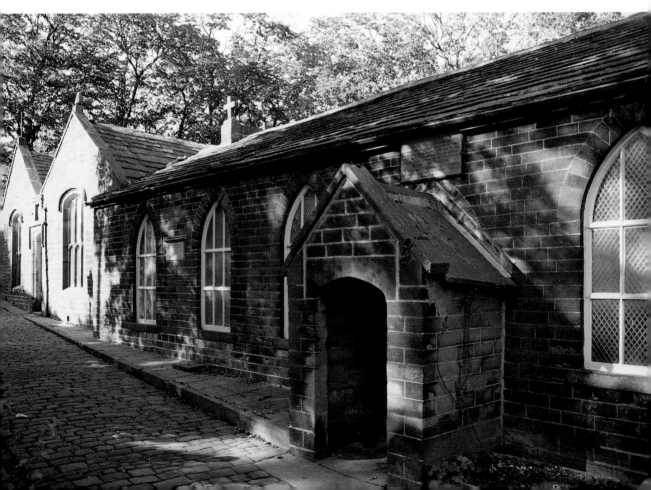

industrial scene a severe shock to the senses. But he was writing before the renaissance of the past 20 years: a General Improvement Area was designated in 1968, the first Calderdale Tourist Centre was set up, and arts and crafts now flourish as never before.

The desolate moorland to the S has an outstanding landmark visible for miles around: Stoodley Pike, started to celebrate the fall of Paris in 1814, and completed a year later at the end of the Napoleonic Wars after Waterloo. It fell down in 1854, coincident with the outbreak of the Crimean War, and was rebuilt in 1856 to commemorate the peace. The Pennine Way comes N from Blackstone Edge, passes Stoodley Pike, crosses the Calder valley, and continues via Colden Vale, Heptonstall Moor and Wadsworth Moor into Brontë country. Here the landscape is wild and bleak, its colours changing subtly with the seasons, its overall darkness brightened in summer by the sharp green of bilberry and the white puffs of cottongrass, and later by the foxy tan of bracken. The many upland reservoirs attract a variety of migrant birds such as Arctic tern and Canada goose, besides resident grey heron, redshank, golden plover and carrion crow, to name but a few. Part of the Pennine Way runs alongside the deep woods and waterfalls in the valley of Hardcastle Crags, all the more delightful by contrast with the enfolding moorland.

Heptonstall Finest village of SW Yorkshire, on a hilltop high above Hebden Bridge. It once commanded the main road from Halifax into Lancashire, in existence long before the valley road constructed in the late 18th century. A few houses date from the 16th century, most are of the 17th and 18th.

During the Civil War Heptonstall was strongly Parliamentarian and suffered fierce skirmishes. Royalists pillaged and set fire to the village, but held it for only

54 Heptonstall is unusual in having two Anglican churches: the older one (mainly 13th and 14th century) was dismantled in 1854, and the ruins now overshadow its Gothic-style replacement. The beautiful 13th-century font is preserved in the new church. The grave of the young American-born poet Sylvia Plath-Hughes (d. 1963) is in the newer part of the churchyard.

55 *Late afternoon in Hebden Bridge.*

three weeks before evacuating Halifax and the whole area in face of the new army coming from Scotland (1644).

The octagonal, later extended, Wesleyan Chapel (1764), whose foundation stone was laid by John Wesley himself on one of his many visits, is thought to be the oldest chapel in continuous use in the world. Its roof was prefabricated in sections and brought by horse and cart from Rotherham. Weavers' Square, on a site of former weavers' cottages, received its present form in 1967, 'a museum of stone', consisting of pavements of every kind to be found in the locality. New House (1763) and Whitehall (1579), both in Northgate, are notable examples of Heptonstall's stylish domestic architecture. A splendid approach to the village is over the moors from Colne (Lancashire), and alongside Hebden Water.

Luddenden Dean The beck which has carved out this narrow glen rises near Oxenhope and runs down between the lonely moorlands of Ovenden and Midgley. The attractive village of Luddenden has hardly changed over two centuries, but it is quiet now – the huge mill has fallen into ghostly disuse, with blocked and broken windows, no noise of work or people.

The Ryburn Valley   Delightful walks through riverside woods or following the line of the disused railway (parallel to the old main road running up the valley from Halifax to Manchester). The Calderdale Way provides here some of the quintessential scenes of West Yorkshire: descending from Norland Moor (above Sowerby Bridge; fine moorland panoramas), it crosses the Ryburn at Ripponden, where the first sight of the oldest part of the village is a stony roofscape. After a slight detour, the medieval packhorse bridge comes into view beside a comfortable inn(**57**) which preserves its original, heavily impressive cruck beams (see p.00).

The hills on both sides of the valley above Ripponden are studded with dams and reservoirs. At Ringstone Edge is the site of a neolithic settlement and stone circle; past Baitings and Blackstone Edge reservoirs (on the road from Ripponden to Rochdale) a hillside path leads up to a remarkably preserved, stone-paved road, certainly medieval, possibly Roman.

The Calderdale Way continues over to Cragg Vale through the lovely village of Millbank, once a weavers' village and now a conservation area reclaimed from a recent period of decline, and in its contours reminiscent of an Italian hill village. This is an area which should be taken slowly for full appreciation of its small, ancient fields and stone walls, its chapels and mills in hamlets such as Soyland and Lumb. Spring comes late in these parts, and in June the meadows are full of buttercups, bluebells and sorrel.

Saltaire   Model industrial village (1850–76) in Shipley Glen, beside the river Aire, on the outskirts of Bradford. It was the enlightened inspiration of Sir Titus Salt (1803–76), and remains virtually complete, an essential visit for any devotee of Victorian life and architecture. Salt made his fortune by introducing long-stapled alpaca and angora into the manufacture of worsteds, thereby producing cloth

56 *Saltaire Mill (1851-3) was designed by Sir William Fairbairn for the philanthropic Bradford wool-master Sir Titus Salt. This is just one side of the massive foursquare building, which covers 7 acres. At one time 3000 workers were employed here, producing up to 30,000 yards of cloth per day. The main chimney is copied from the Santa Maria dei Frari in Venice.*

specially adapted to the needs of Victorian fashion (e.g. crinolines). The terrible conditions in Bradford at this time, with disease and overcrowding and fermenting discontent, determined him on the work which was to take the rest of his life.

His great Italianate mill (1851–3; **56**) was the largest and most advanced in Europe, accommodating the entire process of worsted manufacture under one roof. Special devices in the chimneys reduced air pollution, some of the machinery was installed under floors to eliminate noise, and the huge workrooms were made light and airy by plate-glass windows. Workers' houses were laid out on a grid plan, with piped gas and water, and the crucial innovation of back alleys, in contrast to the insanitary, jerry-built back-to-back housing pertaining elsewhere. Public buildings catered for complete community life – an elaborate Congregational church in classical style, corner shops, schools, a hospital, and an Institute with public rooms and a library (still in use today, and housing an entertaining exhibition of Victorian pipe organs and harmoniums). Sir Titus would allow no public house, pawn shop or police station in Saltaire; on the other hand, he was lavish in entertaining his work-force on special occasions, giving meals for as many as 2000 at his mansion at Crow Nest near Halifax. The houses have been separately owned, independent of the mill, since the 1930s. The mill itself, after various changes of ownership, has finally closed.

57 *The inn at Ripponden, near the packhorse bridge over the Ryburn. Like the bridge, the inn is medieval in origin, and has preserved its massive curving cruck beams. The exterior walls were plain grey stone until recently – white rendering is an innovation in this area.*

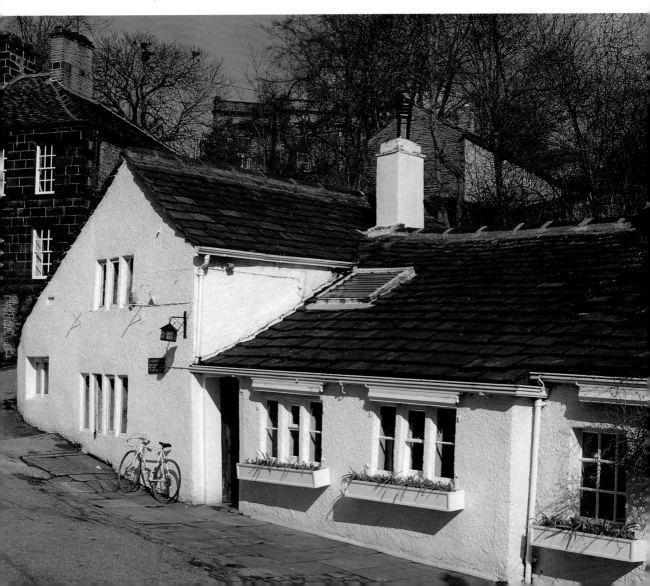

The North York Moors

See map on back endpapers

Bounded to the west by the formidable ramparts of the Cleveland and Hambleton hills, and to the east by the mighty cliffs of one of the finest stretches of England's coast, the north-eastern moorland of Yorkshire has remained relatively unexplored and unspoilt, untouched by any major traffic route, and far from any sizeable town. A few names are generally familiar: Whitby, no longer the prime fishing and ship-building port it once was, but still a favoured holiday resort; Thirsk, noted for horse-racing, and once a stage on the Great North Road; Rievaulx, exquisite remains of a great and ancient abbey; the Cleveland Way and the Lyke Wake Walk, popular routes marked out for the pleasure of long-distance wayfarers (see map on back endpapers). But who has heard of Roseberry Topping, the little conical hill which is such a distinctive landmark? Or of Fryup Dale, or Mount Grace, or Chop Gate, or the surprising sharp-edged amphitheatre of the Hole of Horcum? This is a country still awaiting a Turner to paint its heathery heights, its subtle range of browns as the snows recede, the vivid greens and golds of lawn-like summer valleys; or a Hughes to write the poetry of the near wilderness of high moorland, the sadness of departed industry and lost sailors.

58, 59 *Buttercups catching the early summer light in the peaceful valley of Rosedale* (left) *and the pretty village of Carlton-in-Cleveland* (above). *Like so many villages in this district, Carlton is strung out along a stream crossed by little footbridges; it is sheltered by the steep escarpment of the Cleveland Hills, rising to over 1000 feet.*

The entire area was designated a National Park in 1952. On the north side, the river Esk rises on Westerdale Moor and meanders eastwards to Whitby; the Leven rises on Kildale Moor and wanders even more erratically (generally west and north) to run into the Tees. The south side of the moors is drained by numerous small streams (variously called gill or beck) flowing down to the river Derwent and the Vale of York.

Valleys are deep and secluded, and the rivers scarcely dominate, as they do in the Dales. At first glance the green middle slopes of hillsides networked with dry-stone walls might recall the Dales, but the resemblance soon ends: the moors and wide open hills must first be enjoyed from the heights. For walkers, the Lyke Wake Walk, the Cleveland Way and the Coast to Coast Way (see Swaledale) take in much lovely scenery and are well marked, but it must be emphasised that they are strenuous and require careful preparation. The National Park publishes a good series of Waymark Guides, for shorter rambles, and the Walks for Motorists series is also invaluable.

Roads have to be taken seriously, for they are often dramatically steep. Sutton Bank (the approach from Thirsk) can be perilous, but stopping places at the top give spectacular views south and west. Blakey Bank is another such incline, between Rosedale and Farndale, its highest point a stony desert among lumpy remains of old ironstone mine workings – a poignant contrast with the sylvan beauties of these dales. Farndale is famous for wild daffodils in springtime, strictly guarded in a nature reserve. Many fine drives criss-cross the central moorland, roads snaking up and down, beckoning ever onwards, with sudden sharp descents into secret hollows where a stream may have to be forded (e.g. between Westerdale and Kildale). The Forestry Commission has opened some attractive recreation

73

areas and trails, including the Dalby Forest Drive, near the pretty village of Thornton Dale.

From the low road (A 172) along the National Park border between Thirsk and Stokesley there are fine panoramic views of the Clevelands rising to over 1000 feet. Carlton-in-Cleveland (**59**) is one of the loveliest villages here, strung out along the line of a stream in a pattern characteristic of the North York Moors villages (Thornton Dale, Levisham, Goathland). Hutton-le-Hole is another, much visited, where there is an exceptionally interesting Folk Museum.

Kirkbymoorside, Helmsley and Pickering are small market towns south of the Moors, all with a comfortable air of prosperity, and enhanced by colour livelier than the greys of the Dales. Here the local stone comes lighter, cream, buff or glowing ochre; brick is also evident, and everywhere red pantile roofs weather with considerable subtlety, set off by the smart white paint of doors and small-paned windows. Both Helmsley and Pickering have remains of medieval castles, and the glorious abbeys of Whitby and Rievaulx are national treasures.

The spectacular coast, where beautiful sandy beaches curve between towering headlands, is of special geological interest (see Ravenscar). Constant erosion by wind and wave accounts for a loss rate averaging two inches a year – it sounds little in itself but explains why many a cliff-top cottage has fallen into the sea. Low tide at Robin Hood's Bay lays bare wide stepped platforms or 'scaurs', cut by the waves and undermining the cliffs. In addition, frequent cliff-falls and quarrying have exposed stratified formations of rock going as far back as the Jurassic period, 150 million years ago. This has been a great hunting ground for fossil collectors: dynosaur footprints have been discovered, and many ammonites ranging in size from a pinhead to a 2-foot diameter. Jet is still to be found on the shore near

60, 61 *Harbourside houses at Staithes* (above), *north of Whitby, one of the most picturesque old fishing villages on this part of the coast, and at Robin Hood's Bay* (right). *The formidable cliffs along this north-east coast suffer continual erosion from the remorseless action of waves and weather. Captain Cook first felt the call of the sea at Staithes, where he was apprenticed to a shopkeeper at the age of 16. Parts of the shop are incorporated in 'Cook Cottage', a stage on the Cook Heritage Trail.*

74

Whitby; it was the source of an active industry in the 19th century, when jet jewellery was popular. Alum, once an important ingredient of the dyeing process, was mined from the 17th to the 19th centuries, as was ironstone, further north near Loftus, where there is an interesting mining museum. The only mineral worked nowadays is potash, in a new mine between Staithes and Loftus. It is claimed to be the deepest in Europe (1½ miles), with some segments beneath the sea; on reaching the bottom workers may have to continue a further 18 miles, in considerable heat, along horizontal shafts spreading out like the spokes of a wheel.

62 The startling outline of Roseberry Topping, near Great Ayton, surrounded by Newton Wood and Stacks Wood.

The romantic villages of Staithes and Robin Hood's Bay, resonant with memories of seafaring, Captain Cook, and smuggling, have hardly changed in appearance over the past 200 years, clustering tight against the cliffs, and bravely facing the elements (the Cod and Lobster Inn at Staithes was washed away for the third time in the great storm of 1953). The once proud fishing industry is now almost defunct, apart from small-scale inshore gathering of shellfish.

Inland from Whitby, on Fylingdales Moor, a NATO early-warning radar system stands encased in three white domes visible for miles around. They were built in 1962, and after 25 years service are due to be replaced by a pyramid construction which promises to be an even more outlandish sight than the three 'golf balls'. Such encroachment, along with that of extended agriculture and forestry, has contributed to the depletion of the total National Park area by 25 per cent since its inception.

But we can turn our backs on 'the muck that marks the common man' (Wynford Vaughan-Thomas, p. 218), and lift our eyes to the hills – perhaps to the strange brooding rock pinnacles of the Bridestones on Lockton Low Moor, or the Roman road on Wheeldale Moor, or medieval crosses or paved packhorse causeways. Bird-watchers, naturalists, geologists and archaeologists will all be happy here, as will everyone who enjoys a great variety of superb natural landscape, whether in the blue mists of summer, the silent serenity of winter snows, or best of all the magnificence of its autumn heather.

Danby   At the centre of the national park, where Danby High Moor is traversed by the Lyke Wake Walk. Empty, inhospitable moorland now, though archaeological digs have revealed evidence of human habitation up to 4000 years ago. The Danby Beck rises on the High Moor and runs due N through a narrow, pretty valley to join the Esk near the village. The information, exhibitions and courses of the Danby Lodge Moors Centre provide an excellent introduction to exploration of the whole area.

Farndale see introduction and **Rosedale**

Goathland   Spacious green village through which the Eller Beck runs N to the Esk. W of the village a complex series of gills and becks coming from Egton High Moor and Wheeldale Moor gives rise to captivating scenery and to waterfalls, the biggest of which is the 70-foot Mallyan Spout (about 1 mile W of the village), deservedly popular; the walk to Mallyan Spout and Beck Hole and back to the village is particularly lovely. A mile NW of this is a well-preserved stretch of Roman road, Wade's Causeway, said to be the best in England. Medieval Beggar's Bridge at Glaisdale.

Great Ayton   Attractive little town with good 18th-century houses and a Quaker School (on High Green, near the Cook Museum). It spreads along the banks of the river Leven, which runs SW here and on to Stokesley, handsomest town of NE Yorkshire, before turning N into Teesdale. Great Ayton lies at the foot of the high moorland which shelters its E side and makes a distinctive panorama. One hill is a surprising, separate peak, almost a little volcano, quite unlike the rest of the moorland. From some angles its profile appears to have been gouged away into a sheer cliff – the result of a landslide in the 19th century. This is Roseberry Topping (**62**). It was acquired by the National Trust in 1985 and following a successful appeal for funds, extensive work has begun to repair eroded paths and replant and maintain the mature oak woodlands. Easby Moor, to the SE, is crowned by a monument erected (1827) in memory of Captain Cook, the most renowned of English navigators, who passed his childhood days in Great Ayton. He joined his first trading ship at Whitby in 1746 when he was 18. In 1755 he joined the Royal Navy, and for the next 12 years was principally engaged in surveying the coasts of Canada and Newfoundland, work which brought him to the notice of the Royal Society, which in 1768 invited him to command an expedition to the South Pacific. The three-year voyage in the *Endeavour* was to be his most famous journey: he observed the Transit of Venus at Tahiti, charted the entire coast of New Zealand and that of eastern Australia (claiming it for England and naming it New South Wales), and returned with a vast body of information about the previously unknown lands of the South Pacific collected by the botanist Joseph Banks and accompanying artists. Cook's second voyage round the world lasted from 1772 to 1774. His final and fatal expedition left England in 1776, its purpose to discover a northern sea passage between the Atlantic and Pacific. He was killed on 14 February 1779, in a fracas with natives on Hawaiian island.

The humble house in Great Ayton which was the village school has now on its upper floor a small museum devoted to Cook, with graphic descriptions of the voyages, beautiful model ships, and a good range of books. The cottage where he lived with his parents was removed lock stock and barrel in 1934, to be re-erected in Melbourne; its site is marked by an obelisk. 'Cook Country' is a particular place of pilgrimage for Australian and New Zealand visitors; the Captain Cook Heritage

OVERLEAF
63 *The North York Moors, seen from the Pickering–Whitby road.*

Trail (information displayed on High Green) is a round trip including his birthplace at Marton, and Staithes and Whitby on the coast.

Helmsley A comfortable and welcoming little town, with the red roofs characteristic of this side of Yorkshire, creamy stone and white paint; neat gardens, a stream and trees along Castlegate. On the W side of the market square, a half-timbered cottage (16th–17th century) has been joined to two Georgian houses to form a popular hotel, the Black Swan. Helmsley is dominated by its castle (originally 12th century), of which little remains apart from three sides of the 14th-century keep, pierced by round-headed window spaces, unusually elegant. The best view is from E to W in the morning, with the sunlight from the S striking the graceful tower.

Hutton-le-Hole Stone-built cottages (late 17th century) ranged either side of the Hutton Beck running SE towards Ryedale are set off by wide, open greens and pretty white fences (**65**). Sheep-farming was important here in the Middle Ages, as elsewhere in Yorkshire; later, flax was grown, and weaving flourished in the early 18th century. Other industries have come and gone over the centuries. One, perhaps surprising, was due to an influx of Huguenot glassmakers in the late 1500s, but this was short lived, and the skill was not passed on to the locals. There were later and longer-lasting enterprises in lime-burning, and coal- and iron-mining (see p.86). Land use now is almost entirely pastoral, devoted to sheep.

The Ryedale Folk Museum (founded 1964) in the middle of the village is a place of the most absorbing interest. The entrance buildings, part of an 18th-century farm, show the tools and equipment pertaining to various bygone local trades, such as tannery and thatching, and the manage of heavy horses. 2½ acres of open ground behind the museum include a craftshops block housing old-style trades,

64 *Wild flowers at Helmsley Castle, a 12th-century fortification whose 14th-century keep is the dominant feature of the attractive town of Helmsley, on the southern edge of the moors.*

e.g. clogmaking, tinsmithery, and an iron foundry, besides separate reconstructed cottages brought from surrounding villages. The basic plan and building method of the ancient cruck house is clearly explained. Not all buildings are reconstructed: the crofter's cottage and the barn are examples of local types built according to archaeological evidence. A unique exhibit is a glassmakers' furnace from Elizabethan days, excavated in 1969.

Kirkdale   2 miles W of Kirkbymoorside, a secluded place with a little church, St Gregory's Minster, almost hidden among yews and cypresses in an extensive churchyard in this valley which seems so remote from the world – one of the approach roads crosses a ford where the water sometimes runs 3 feet deep.

The church is of Saxon origin and may have been founded in the latter half of the 7th century; Saxon coffin lids are preserved within the church. The inscription in Northumbrian English on the sundial over the S porch dates the oldest existing parts of the church precisely between 1055 and 1065. It tells that the church was rebuilt 'anew from the ground' in the days of Edward the King (Edward the Confessor, crowned 1043, died 1066) and of Tosti(g) the Earl (who became Earl of Northumberland in 1055, and died in 1066 at the battle of Stamford Bridge). The unusually high, narrow W door is typical of this late Anglo-Saxon period. The sundial is the best example of its kind to be found. It has a horizontal line for sunrise and sunset, and a vertical one for midday; morning and afternoon are divided into four parts. The gnomon or marker is missing.

Lastingham   St Mary's church has the only crypt in England with a rounded apse (**66**). Most powerful in atmosphere and virtually unchanged in appearance since the time it was built, *c.* 1080, the undecorated apse arch springs straight from the ground. A monastery was founded here in the mid-7th century, and the

81

Venerable Bede gives an account of it in his *Ecclesiastical History* (731). Probably it was destroyed at some time during the Danish invasions (9th and 10th centuries), and the crypt was built as a shrine to the memory of the founder, St Cedd, Bishop of Northumberland, who was buried here.

Mount Grace Priory   Near the attractive village of Osmotherley, lying close to the W escarpment of the Cleveland hills on a sheltered slope bright in springtime with flowering cherry, bluebells and campion, its tranquillity hardly disturbed by the noise of the nearby main road.

The Priory was founded in 1398, the last but one of the seven English monasteries of the Carthusian Order (founded by St Bruno at La Grande Chartreuse in France). Members of this order were obliged to live and study in complete ascetic solitude, not living as a community as did the monks of abbeys such as Fountains. Each monk had a separate dwelling and garden. The great cloister on the N side of the church is surrounded by walls in which the doorways and food-hatches of these 'cells' are clearly visible; there are further traces of cells in the smaller cloister S of the church. The church itself was quite small and relatively plain, with adjoining chapter house, refectory (only used on feastdays) and prior's cell.

The Dissolution brought an end to the priory as such in 1539, and it passed into private ownership. Buildings N of the gatehouse are still a private house. The ruins were excavated and partially reconstructed around 1900. Owned by the National Trust since 1953, they are cared for by English Heritage.

Pickering   On the S side of the Moors, a pleasant market town which makes a good centre for exploring E Yorkshire, within easy reach of the coast and of York. Its 13th-century castle (now in ruins) was built on an artificial mound (a motte) NE of the town centre, and commands good views. More dominant is the parish church, approached up a stepped pathway leading from the market place (once the village green). It dates from the mid-12th century, but its architecture is complicated and considerably restored. The mid-15th-century wall paintings, however, are one of the most complete series remaining in England (restored 1880), depicting mainly Biblical events in lively naïve style; the outlines are clear, and colours subdued, predominantly blue-black and indian red. The modern (1911) Roman Catholic church in Potter Hill can be visited, if closed, on application at the presbytery next door. Its sculpted octagonal font is the work of Eric Gill (1882–1940); on the side panels stylised foliage alternates with figurative scenes, the most appealing being a St Joseph, with his carpenter's tools, bending tenderly over a calm but independent Child.

Beck Isle Museum, in a late-18th-century house facing the bridge (W of the market place), houses a good collection showing local history and rural life.

Pickering is the S terminus of the North Yorkshire Moors Railway; steam trains run up to Grosmont (an hour's journey), where connection can be made with Whitby. Originally engineered by Stevenson, it goes through some of the best of moorland scenery, and stations at Levisham, Newtondale Halt and Goathland enable passengers to explore on foot the most delectable of woods and valleys.

Ravenscar   Spectacular coastal area with some of the highest cliffs of the whole E coast, where the Romans had a look-out station. A geological trail of about 3 miles (described in a National Trust booklet) begins in the village and in part follows the track of the disused Scarborough to Whitby railway. It is interesting on account of geological faults and erosion from the old days of alum-mining and from the sea, and also for the abundance of marine bird-life.

Rievaulx (67)   Glorious ruins of a once glorious Cistercian abbey founded here in 1131 under Abbot William, who had been secretary to the founder of the order, St

66 The crypt at St Mary's, Lastingham, is reached by a flight of steps in the middle of the nave (well restored with fitting simplicity in 1879). The main body of the crypt is square, with a nave and aisles, rounded early Norman arches, and low vaulting supported by four immense squat pillars whose capitals, starkly decorated, are at eye level. There is no other crypt like this in England.

67 *Rievaulx Abbey ruins: a view through the 13th-century north arcade of the choir, where the raised area indicates the site of the high altar. Part of the monastic buildings, including the chapter house, can be seen beyond.*

Bernard of Clairvaux. Its rapid rise to prosperity soon made it one of the principal parent foundations in Britain (it pre-dates Fountains), with all its buildings complete by the end of the 1200s, when the community had grown to 140 monks and at least 500 lay brethren under Abbot (later Saint) Aeldred.

Rievaulx – the name means the valley of the Rye – has after Fountains the most complete abbey remains in England, every bit as exquisite as Fountains, even airier and more delicate, and perhaps more easily comprehensible. The river was diverted from the E side of the valley to provide Rievaulx with more meadow land. The constricted site accounts for the N–S alignment of the church, instantly and surprisingly apparent from the visitors' entrance. The high altar is at the S end, and true E is described as the ecclesiastical N, in admirably cavalier fashion.

The original grandeur of English Gothic can be envisaged with no difficulty, most expecially in the church with its impressive proportions and tiered ranges of windows. Traces of ceramic mosaic tile flooring and reconstructed fragments of arcading in the cloisters suggest a certain elegance. The Historic Buildings and Monuments Commission (English Heritage) cares for Rievaulx, and the visitors' tour is carefully laid out and excellently explained.

At the Dissolution (1539) the abbey, together with Helmsley Castle, was given to the Earls of Rutland, absentee landlords to whom must be owed the completeness of what remains – there was no conversion to a house, and apparently little systematic removal of the stone. It later passed to the Duncombe family, whose fortune came from the lucrative hereditary post of Registrar-General of Excise, and from the favour of Charles II. The house at Duncombe Park (started 1713), adjacent to Rievaulx, has had a chequered history, and was until recently a school.

Rievaulx Terrace was acquired by the National Trust in 1963. It is reached by a steep lane up from Rievaulx village, first through woods starry with flowers of wild garlic in springtime, and then by a winding path of less than 1 mile through woodland originally planted by the creator of the terrace, Thomas Duncombe III, around 1760. He was perhaps vying with Aislabie's landscaping at Fountains, but with such a different approach and conception, and such different raw material, as to produce something unique in man-made naturalness. The terrace, a sweep of mown grass about 125 feet wide, curves gently above a cliff with hanging woods. The trees have been cut away at intervals to reveal new sights of the abbey below, every view more enchanting than the last, and always with a backdrop of village, woods, and moorland. At either end of the terrace stands a temple, one round, domed and colonnaded after the Tuscan temple of Vesta at Tivoli, and the other Ionic, recently restored, its interior lavishly painted and carved in classical style – Duncombe used it for summer dinner parties *in villeggiatura* (there was a kitchen below, now a museum). The temples are understated, almost retiring into the trees to leave the stage entirely to the principal character, Rievaulx Abbey.

Robin Hood's Bay (61, 68)   One of the most picturesque fishing villages of the entire coast, only to be rivalled by Staithes (**60**), N of Whitby. Cars must be left at the cliff top before the steep walk down to the little harbour and clustering red-roofed houses.

A stone beside the car-park is a forceful reminder of the severity of life on this coast until recent times, and of 'the dogged determination of the people of Whitby, Hawsker and Robin Hood's Bay'. When on 18 January 1881 the brig *Visitor* ran aground here, the lifeboat had to be brought overland from Whitby 6 miles away, on a road rising to 500 feet and through 7-foot snowdrifts. 200 men cleared the road ahead of it, and it was dragged by 18 horses on tow lines. It was launched here two hours after leaving Whitby, and the brig's crew was saved at the second attempt.

Many houses have red pantiles, stone facings, and brick in a herringbone pattern characteristic of these parts; their special charm owes much to the narrowness, and indeed congestion, of the stepped and cobbled alleyways between them. Some houses actually overhang King's Beck, which flows down through the village. There are many tales of smuggling, rife until well into the 19th century – it was said that bolts of silk, tea and liquor could be carried from the shore to the top of the village without seeing the light of day, and it is certain that many houses had interconnecting cellars, or cupboards whose doors opened two ways into adjoining houses.

The NE-coast coble , the sturdy fishing boat designed for launching in heavy surf from a rocky beach, can still be seen. It has a high bow, flat bottom with no keel, and flat sharply sloping stern; often brightly painted, as in the old days, but now invariably motorised, no longer under sail.

Rosedale   Quiet, lovely valley (**58**) running due S from the high moors of Westerdale and Danby. Impressive views, especially from the top of Blakey Bank towards Farndale. Ralph Cross at Rosedale Head, now adopted as the emblem of the National Park, is one of the few remaining stone crosses erected as guide posts in the Middle Ages. There are distinct traces on the higher slopes of railway tracks which served the ironstone industry during its short-lived prosperity in the mid-19th century, tracks which now afford some pleasant walks. Lime-kiln remains on Rosedale Bank Top.

Rosedale Abbey was a small nunnery founded in the early 12th century. Nothing remains of it in the village of the same name, apart from a buttress and part of a spiral staircase; extensive ruins were swept away when the new church was built in 1839. It is a pretty, compact village at the head of the lower dale, which is gently wooded with small forestry plantations.

Thirsk   Market town of the Vale of York lying just E of the Great North Road, the gateway to the Moors, which are approached via the dramatic escarpment of Sutton Bank.

The fine Perpendicular parish church of St Mary (in Kirkgate, off the market square) is the best of its kind in North Yorkshire and bears comparison with the great churches of Suffolk of the same period. Magnificent tower arch and wagon roof. Striking ranges of generously wide windows in the clerestory and on the ground floor. Exterior walls finished with pierced battlements. The little window over the S porch is that of a room where a hermit lived in the 16th century. The Jesus Bell (1410), the oldest in the tower, was brought here from Fountains Abbey after the Dissolution (1539).

Whitby   Until recent times an important fishing and ship-building port at the mouth of the river Esk. The harbour, where a statue commemorates Captain Cook (see p.77), is sheltered by a high cliff promontory, on which the abbey ruins (**70**) and the parish church stand like protecting guardians.

An Anglo-Saxon abbey was established during the 7th century by St Hilda, a Northumbrian princess early converted to Christianity and inspired by St Aidan, founder of the monastery on the Holy Island of Lindisfarne. The fact that the Synod of Whitby was convened here in 663 (see p.45), to effect conciliation between the Celtic and Roman churches and to find an agreed formula for deciding the date of Easter, testifies to the quickly established religious importance of the place under Hilda's rule. Its sudden flowering was more beautifully expressed in the poems of Caedmon, who started as a farm-hand in Hilda's time and was educated in the abbey. Several mystical Anglo-Saxon poems, notably the *Dream of the Rood* and the *Harrowing of Hell*, are attributed to him. A charming footnote to the life of St Hilda is her legendary ability to turn snakes into stone. Quantities of ammonites have been discovered here, and three of these coiled fossils appear on the town's coat of arms,

68 *Low tide at Robin Hood's Bay, showing the rocky ledges or 'scaurs' cut by the tide, a fruitful hunting ground for sea anemones, ammonites and crabs. The cliff paths here (part of the Cleveland Way) may be strenuous and, in places, treacherous, but the intrepid walker is rewarded by a wealth of geological complexity and wildlife.*

each with the head of a snake.

St Hilda's abbey was destroyed by the Danish invaders, and refounded for the Benedictine order in the 11th century. The buildings we see now belong to the 12th and 13th centuries – a powerful, unforgettable ruin on its bare headland backed by ever-changing skies and seascape, so different from the green valleys and sophisticated landscaping of Rievaulx or Fountains.

The Norman parish church was the abbey church and is right beside it. 'A wonderful jumble of medieval and Georgian when one walks round it', says Pevsner, 'but when one enters it, hard to believe and impossible not to love.' It is dominated by a triumphant three-decker pulpit, and is claimed to be the only Anglican church in the world with no altar, only a communion table, and this eccentricity is compounded by the fact that the rood screen is actually the family pew of the local gentry, who could enter from outside by a private staircase.

The Whitby-born novelist Storm Jameson (1891-1986) says that the soul of an old ship inhabits this church. 'Ships' carpenters put up the present roof, and the windows under it are so like cabin windows that on the rare Sundays when we occupied my grandfather's pew in one of the galleries I could only dream of voyages. Outside, the dust of Saxons, Danes, monks, ship-builders, master mariners, lies deep under the rank grass between wrinkled gravestones eaten by the salt' (*Journey from the North*, 1969). Many memorials tell of shipwrecks and of Whitby people lost at sea.

Like other places along this coast, Whitby has been subjected to constant and relentless erosion. The Irish novelist Bram Stoker found it fascinating enough to set part of his best-selling vampire extravaganza here – the famous *Dracula* (1897), in which he makes much of gravestones perched above crumbling precipices, of lurid

69 *The long climb of 199 steps from the harbour up to Whitby Abbey is well worth the effort for the view of town, sea and distant cliffs. (There is a back way, a motor road, but that would be cheating.)*

70 *The drama of Whitby Abbey is mightily reinforced by its cliff-top site, where it braves the elements with inspiring fortitude.*

thunderstorms, and of the perils of sleepwalking at the cliff edge. Currently there are signs of a Dracula revival, with an eye to the tourist trade; one awaits the arrival of the Draculaburger.

Tourism has been part of Whitby's economy for well over a century, and it was a favoured haunt of writers and artists. Two town trails (one for either side of the town) describe walks of about an hour, and enable the visitor to enjoy all the pleasures of bridges and shipyards, medieval streets and alleyways, buildings Georgian, Victorian and modern – all close and compact, and still, in spite of recent growth, very much integral to the North Yorkshire scene.

Let Storm Jameson have the last word:

Not a great way beyond the upper harbour, the hills begin to fold in; a few miles inland they rise to a wide stretch of moor, by turns fox-red, purple, bone-grey, seamed to runnels by peaty water and narrow valleys filled with foxgloves, gorse, dog-roses, thyme, bracken, and a few self-possessed villages. In my childhood the moor road from Pickering to Whitby said all there is to say about the instinct for solitude, sharper than the instinct to herd: peewits, sea-gulls, a few grouse, and at a certain point, the first sight, piercing the heart, of the church and the Abbey clinging to the East cliff.

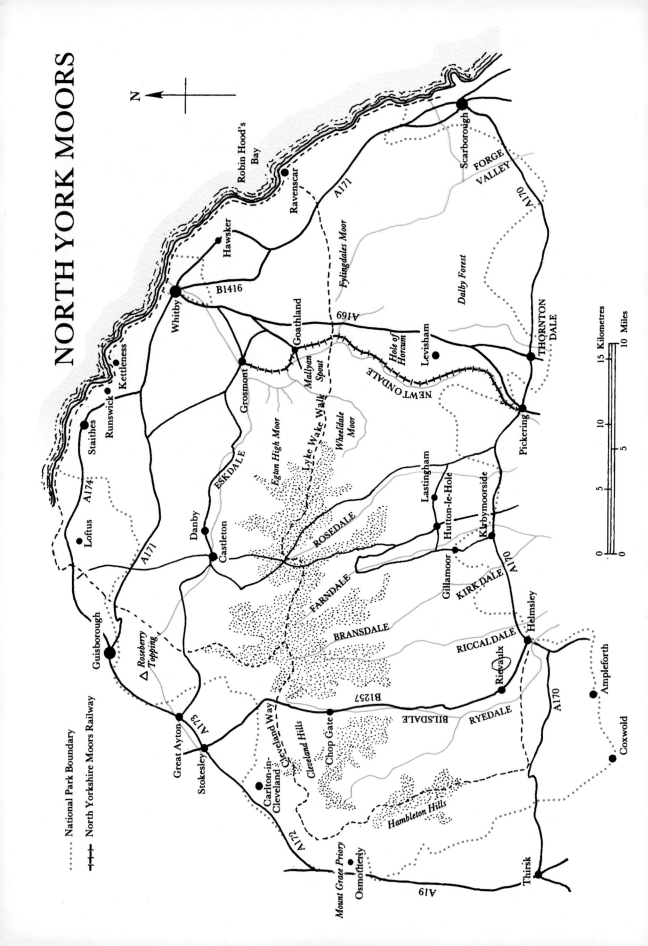